Peter Howden

The Horse

How to Buy and Sell

Peter Howden

The Horse

How to Buy and Sell

ISBN/EAN: 9783744669856

Printed in Europe, USA, Canada, Australia, Japan

Cover: Foto ©Lupo / pixelio.de

More available books at **www.hansebooks.com**

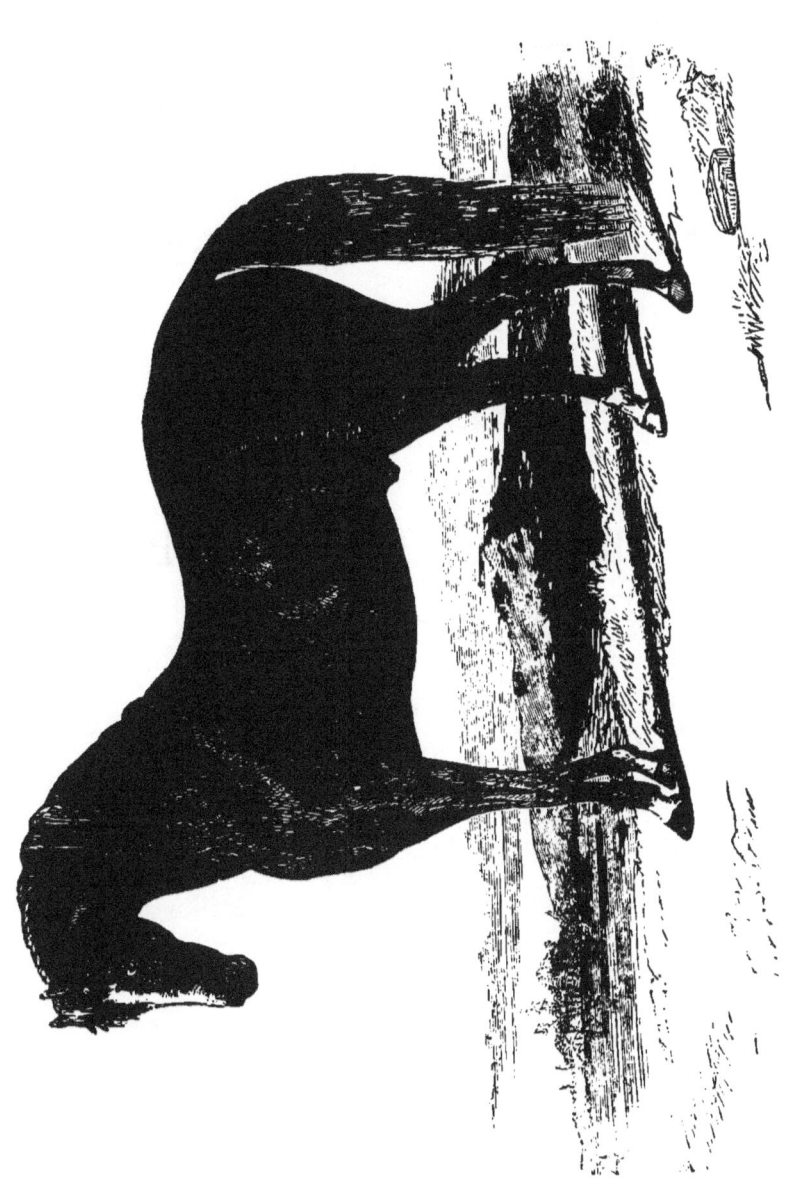

[Frontispiece.]

THE HORSE;

HOW TO BUY AND SELL.

GIVING THE POINTS WHICH DISTINGUISH A

SOUND FROM AN UNSOUND HORSE.

BY
PETER HOWDEN.

NEW YORK:
ORANGE JUDD COMPANY,
751 BROADWAY.
1882.

Entered, according to Act of Congress, in the year 1882, by the
ORANGE JUDD COMPANY,
In the Office of the Librarian of Congress, at Washington.

PUBLISHERS' PREFACE.

The rapidly growing fondness among both sexes for Horses in the United States, is very naturally developing a desire for knowledge regarding the points and characteristics of this noble animal. Hitherto this knowledge has been confined to few. The present volume abounds in general information, stated in so clear and simple a manuer as to enable every one to intelligently buy and sell a horse.

PREFACE.

The object of the present work is to explain, in the simplest manner, what constitutes a sound and what an unsound horse; to note doubtful points, and such things as operate against the proper development of the animal in all parts; and further, as an "unsound horse" is often less dangerous and more useful than the common acceptation of the word "unsound" would imply, I shall take pains to distinguish real from imaginary defects.

To recapitulate the objects of this little treatise, they are—

1. To ascertain what constitutes strict soundness in the horse.
2. To note deviations from soundness unimportant except as to their effect on the market value of the animal.
3. General observations on used horses.

As, of necessity, these subjects sometimes run into each other, a copious index at the end of this book will save the reader any perplexity, and enable him to find what he wants.

There have from time to time been published plenty of books upon the real and imaginary perfections of the horse; but it must be admitted that no horse ever came up to the standard of excellence set up by the authors of these works. Of course not. These writers have brought together a collection of equine excellences, and made it appear to the general reader that a sound and good horse possesses them all. Such argument is not based on common sense. As well expect to find the average human form as divinely beautiful as the Apollo Belvidere or the Venus de Medici; or, at least, to reject as models for the student in sculpture or painting all subjects not "thoroughly up to the mark." Nobody, nothing, is perfect according to our own artificial standards; but with a little attention to practical detail, as laid down by men of experience, and a large allowance of common sense, we may find the tools for our work.

There are few horses that would stand the strict test of examination for purposes of unqualified warranty, even among those that have not been worked; but few indeed would be those that had been worked that would not fall under the denomination of unsound.

One of the most experienced men in the business, who dealt for many years in horses for those who can and will have the best animals in the country, said, "Not one in three of fresh unused horses would pass an examination; and when a horse has reached five years without work, reject him. Do not trouble yourself to find out what it is, there is certainly something wrong about the brute." My experience bears out this counsel. In quadrupeds and men destined to labor, there must be some inherent deficiency in them if they go long without work.

It should be borne in mind that, even where "price is no object," the purchaser cannot insure the possession of a perfect animal, according to any abstract standard. There are very few really bad horses, and, providing horses are properly "placed," that is, put to their right use— the use to which nature fitted them—all difficulties in dealing in horse-flesh will vanish. There is not a grain of sense or truth in the assertion that the horses of to-day are far inferior to the "well-bred horse of old." Again, exceptions do not always prove the rule, and the references to one or more old beauties amongst a lot of young and not beautiful animals go for nothing; or prove no more than that the favorites of older days were not over-worked. Horses not over-worked improve in beauty from eight to sixteen years. During that period the cartilage becomes absorbed, the head smaller and sharper in outline; the prominent bones and tissues again present a youthful roundness, the legs become fine, and the tendons acquire a sharp, well-defined appearance; the horse himself might be taken by a good judge to be much younger than in reality he is, did not his mouth bear evidence to the contrary. The connoisseur, however, rarely needs the evidence of the mouth, the general shape and contour of the horse being in most cases sufficient.

It may be some consolation to those whose knowledge or rather predilection for certain horses is derived from books, to learn that large "users" very rarely obtain exactly such horses as they would choose, they therefore adopt the wise course of balancing one thing with another, and purchase the best they can get.

The present Duke of Wellington recently observed of a horse:— "A great many faults might be found with his hocks; he could not pass an examination. But I do not mind, I know well enough he is a good wearer, and I will give you a cheque for him." The duke's observation proved him to be a practical horseman; in short, a good judge. Horses are essentially animals for use, and although the whole modern system of breeding and training tends to produce animals compactly built and beautiful to look upon, still no amount of training will conceal from the practised eye the features useful or useless for the purpose in view.

THE HORSE; HOW TO BUY AND SELL.

When the extensive and widely ramified trade in horses is considered, the prevailing ignorance of the public as to the laws both physical and civil, relating to their soundness or unsoundness, is a matter of surprise.

Many people appear to think that such knowledge is confined to the larger dealers and proprietors, so that, when a private individual—though a really bad judge of horse-flesh—succeeds in selling, most innocently, a horse that a short time afterwards becomes lame, he immediately acquires the reputation of being "a knowing one" —" a deep hand;" etc.

It is hoped this little work will aid in protecting both buyer and seller from useless litigation. It will be my aim both to free the Warranty from the fallacious security with which it too often invests the purchaser, and to remove the bugbear terrors that surround the seller and too often prevent his obtaining a proper value for a horse. From not knowing the extent of liabilities incurred by the warranty, he is led from motives of prudence, to decline warranting even horses that are sound. I shall also show when a horse should not be rejected because he is unsound, and why, frequently, a sound horse should be avoided.

The late Professor Coleman used to say, "any deviation from nature is an unsoundness." The opinions of most writers, since his time, embrace the same doctrine. To differ from the learned professor altogether would be presumptuous; although, I think, whilst he put his meaning into short and quaint language that it might be easily understood, he calculated upon its receiving a liberal construction. Still, however, the professor considered the above definition of unsoundness a neat and concise explanation of a difficult subject.

The exceptions may not be very numerous with regard to strict soundness, but there may, nevertheless, be many deviations from nature which, instead of impeding the animal functions, are of great service in adapting domesticated animals to the artificial state in which they have to live. Let us take an illustration. The hands of the artisan or laborer, rendered coarse and hard by his daily vocations, must be considered a deviation from nature; but a man with delicate hands, who occasionally goes boating, is aware, from the blisters he gets on his hands, of the convenience and comfort of a more horny texture of skin.

If it were customary for people, upon being taken into any kind of employment, to be "warranted," could a man with these hard hands be warranted sound, *i. e.*, in a natural state, or capable of doing his work properly? Nevertheless, though deviating from nature, the horny hand is the best adapted to hard work.

If the hands of a man had never done hard manual labor, but had always been employed in writing, his skin would remain unaltered, thin, and tender, and he would be adjudged sound, in consequence of his not deviating from nature; but his hands must undergo an alteration of structure before he could earn his food by plowing or digging. It is not, therefore, the training alone, but the altered structure consequent thereon, that is required; yet no one will deny that the adapted structure is the most valuable for performing the requisite labor. Deviations equally slight or unimportant should not vitiate a warranty in horse-flesh. Such vitiation is, however, often attempted, leading to enormous expense, tedious litigation, and frequently the breaking-up of long-established friendships, every one of which evils might be easily prevented by a thorough understanding of the subject I would elucidate. The works on the soundness and unsoundness of horses that have hitherto come under my notice have been, for the most part, compilations or references to cases that have been litigated, which cases, instead of being of any value or service to those unacquainted with the structure and habits of the horse, have only served to mystify them.

WARRANTY.

It has been almost universally supposed that a warranty extends to a definite period. Some imagine that, if anything happens to render a horse unsound during the first month after purchase, the horse can be returned. Others extend the period, and, when told that the warranty does not go forward, but, on the contrary, back from the time of its date, want to know the use of such a document.

USE OF WARRANTY.

The following are the advantages to be derived from the possession of a warranty. Suppose a horse should become ill or diseased within such a reasonable time after purchase as to lead to the belief that the ailment, in all probability, had been caught prior to the sale of the animal, then it could be returned as unsound, because it did not fulfil the conditions of the warranty at the time it was given. Or suppose, within a few days after the purchase has been made, the horse becomes lame, and it is possible to prove that the lameness existed prior to the change of ownership, and that the horse had not been used, as is generally the case with horses of his class, for six weeks after his cure, then the animal is returnable. A horse, therefore, that is turned out to grass after having been afflicted with lameness (unless it can be proved that he has been out for a very considerable period, and that he has been sound during a portion of that time), cannot properly be warranted as sound, and is returnable if he becomes unsound in the part affected before.

Provided that the animal had been properly used according to his class and condition, and that no lameness takes place within a month after he commences work, whether in the service of his new or his late owner, the warranty would cease at the end of a month. The safest way, therefore, is not to warrant the horse until he has been at least six weeks at ordinary work after a perfect cure has been effected.

As there are some physicians who assert that nobody is perfectly sane, and that every one is insane upon one topic or another, so there will be found enlightened veterinarians who assert that there are no sound horses. Certainly not, if they have ever done a day's work. If the slightest deviation from the state in which the colt was, prior to beginning work, is to be significant of unsoundness, I grant that with used horses they are right. The hard condition of the working horse, which really is the cause of his endurance, is, according to this dictum, an unsoundness; because the very work necessary to produce this desired condition will in most cases effect some slight alteration of structure.

Nor is the charge of the veterinary surgeon respecting unsoundness much less deserving of censure. Horses were made for the use of man; and many of the deviations from nature brought on by that use, so far from causing inconvenience to the animal, assist him in the work he has to do. Are we not justified, then, in attributing certain alterations in the structure of animals to the goodness of nature, rather than in questioning their soundness when such alteration, instead of being detrimental, is for their benefit?

Taking substantially, however, Professor Coleman's comprehensive definition of warranty for my text, I will proceed to give a list of the most usual causes for rejecting warranted horses; distinguishing those marks or peculiarities which are really only blemishes from those which do render the animal unsound; and, to make the work as complete as possible, I will endeavor to make clear the vices of the horse, with their attendant consequences.

EXAMINATION.

On the horse being led out of the stable, it is usual to walk up to his withers to ascertain if he is of the required height, as there is generally a difference between the apparent measure in the stable and that taken out of doors, arising from the want of level in the stall.

Next, you should stand before the middle of the chest, to see whether there is any difference in the size of the two fore-feet.

THE FEET.

CONTRACTION.

Contractions, whether arising from original malformation or from subsequent lameness, are by many pronounced unsound. Others admit, where no inconvenience arises from a naturally small foot, that it does not constitute an unsoundness. Why should feet naturally small or narrow at the heels, caused by being reared on high, dry, or hard soil, be pronounced unsound?

Nature has made the small foot as perfect as the larger one. The inside, or sensitive foot, is not too large for the horny case, nor has it with difficulty been squeezed into the case; but the hard, horny case fits the inside with perfect ease. Where contraction is the cause of lameness, it usually arises from changing a natural state of living to one that is artificial. The heat or dryness of the stable is one of the principal causes of contraction, as it aggravates the inflammation produced by work and by the stimulating nature of the food.

Reason, therefore, would suggest that the horse reared in the softest and wettest ground, and having the largest-sized foot, would be most likely to receive injury from the change; and so it has proved in innumerable cases. Great attention and care may keep such feet moderately sound for a short time; but they become crippled almost as soon as they are worked. Not so with the naturally smaller but harder hoof, which has been accustomed to something nearer to the stable dryness; it is not, therefore, from this cause, so soon inflamed. Horses with small hard feet have less fatty membrane to carry, having generally been reared on hard dry grounds. Food not being so plentiful in these situations as on the moist, soft, and fertile plains, they have had to travel farther for it; deriving much good from the exercise thereby induced, and especially from the dry and bracing air of more hilly regions. Horses whose hoofs are naturally small and hard are, therefore, better prepared in every way for the treatment they have to undergo in their apprenticeship to work. They have less useless weight of their own to carry; they are already accustomed to hard dry ground, and to more violent exercise. Horses with small hoofs are more moderate in their action: their feet are not subject to violent inflammation. When inflammation does take place, it is usually slow, and some time elapses before it produces lameness; with a little care they are generally kept in health, and must be pronounced to be   SOUND.

OPEN HOOFS.

The larger-footed horse has more useless weight of his own, not only from having been accustomed to wet, low situations, but also from having had, when young, a greater abundance of food. From having had less exercise, and from the heavy atmosphere having induced quiet, the horn of his hoof has become thin, soft, and weak. The action of this class of horse is high, which is peculiarly bad for the shape of his feet. This habit has been partly acquired through his having been obliged in marshy situations to clear his feet from the soil; but in some horses bred on plains it arises from the position of the shoulder.

It must be obvious to every one, that bringing these horses into dry stables, and making them work upon hard and dry ground, aggravated by their high action, does a greater violence to them than to the small-footed animal; and, as a natural consequence, a very little work produces serious inflammation, pumice-sole, and sometimes perpetual lameness.

These diseases are not merely the result of neglect; they are induced by putting the horse to a kind of work for which he is totally unfitted.

The large-hoofed horse, certainly in his earlier years, should be put to moderate if not slow work, with as little weight upon his back as possible.

FLAT FOOT.

Where the sole of the foot is large and flat, and slightly convex, and where the heels are open, it is often mistaken for a good open foot, even though the **horny covering** is too thin and soft. Such a foot will not stand much work; but if its peculiarities are not the result of disease, the foot may be considered SOUND.

PERFECT FOOT.

The intermediate foot, that is, a foot between the contracted and open one, may be deemed perfection; but, as this degree of excellence is rarely met with, we must be satisfied with that which is the nearest approach to it.

PUMICE SOLE.

If the sole of the foot is in the slightest degree convex, or lower at the middle than at the sides, it may be inferred that the horse has had inflammation of the foot, which has divided some of the laminæ that attach the inner foot to the horny covering. These laminæ, which are one thousand in number, in the healthy foot support the entire weight of the horse, as it were, on springs, instead of letting it rest on the sole alone. In the early stage of inflammation but few of these laminæ are injured. The presence of pumice-sole stamps the horse as UNSOUND.

THE KNEES.

Upon the spotless purity of the knees too much stress is often laid, but security alone is the object to be considered. A properly-formed horse, with his fore and hind quarters proportioned to each other, and his action straight and true, will not fall, except from over fatigue. Here do not deceive yourself, but take care, that in proportion to the beauty or length of the hind quarters be also the obliquity or slanting of the shoulder-blades. The wither has nothing to do with this—so far as regards thinness, height, and other fancies—but it is best when thick at the lower part next the back. A horse thus chosen, with broken knees, unless the tendon is injured, is safer and better, if he has decent hind quarters, than one having upright shoulders, high withers, and all the popular requisites, even with the most immaculately-covered knees. Depend upon it he will have broken knees before he is eight years old. If he escapes it till then, it is a clear proof that he has never been tried; for the first time he is so, down he will be sure to drop.

When your chief desire is that your horse should not fall, care less about the length and beauty of the hind quarters than the proper form of the fore ones, unless price is no object, when you may have the nearer approximation to perfection. Upright shoulders are not of much consequence in harness, as the weight of draught assists the balance.

The mere cutting of the skin, without further injury, does not render the horse weaker on his legs than he was before the accident. You may be assured that he was as frightened at falling as his rider; and the only mischief he has done is in having decreased, not his working, but his market, price.

BROKEN KNEES.

Should the horse at any time have been wounded by falling, the injury he has sustained is to be taken into consideration.

If he has been down at all, even though the skin has not been broken, there will always remain a scurf under the hair, which, to the practised eye, is easily perceptible.

Where this is all the damage he has sustained, he is neither unsound nor blemished.

Where there is an obvious scar from a cut of the skin, it is evidence of a broken knee, let the accident have occurred when or how it may; never heed the excuses offered, take it for granted that it was done against the animal's will, by coming in contact with the ground. This state of broken knee is sound, and the mark a blemish only, provided it is healed over and the skin formed. Prior to this state of perfect cure, from the time of the accident the horse is UNSOUND.

Should the injury, however, have been sufficient to divide the extensor tendon, or otherwise impede or alter the action of the animal, although the part is healed over, he is UNSOUND.

SWOLLEN KNEES.

Another case of injured, though not always broken, knees, may as well be mentioned; that is, where they are swollen: the horse is then UNSOUND.

Where they are of a wenny, or capped, or callous nature, neither increasing nor diminishing, nor requiring extra care, and the action or work of the horse is not interfered with, the horse is SOUND.

But, if the wenny, capped, or callous feature is very conspicuous, it is a blemish, and, where it interferes with the action or work, the horse is UNSOUND.

THE EYES.

The eyes require a very careful examination, as on their proper action our safety and comfort in the use of the animal mainly depend.

A horse with perfect eyes never shies, unless from mismanagement and savage cruelty; and even then he may be cured. He may look at various objects, and, when fresh from want of exercise, he is likely enough to play and frisk on observing different things, particularly such things as pass him quickly; but he may, nevertheless, be perfectly free from vice.

It is absolutely necessary that good light should be obtained, in order to inspect the eyes, and care should be taken that the animal be kept quiet for a sufficient time to enable you to observe these organs narrowly and collectedly. The light best suited for this purpose is that which comes from above, and above only, like that which proceeds from a lantern roof, as in picture-galleries and in some riding-schools. The next best light comes from the skylight common in the latter, or in a covered ride with a light above. Having placed the horse immediately under the light, you will be able to see and examine every defect as clearly as though you were looking at a piece of crystal. The best position one can generally adopt is to put his head in the stable-door, placing yourself in the shade, inside the stable, and looking through one of the eyes with great care, towards the light. When satisfied with the inspection, proceed with equal deliberation and pains to examine the other eye. Now stand opposite the animal's face, and examine both eyes well, by looking through them towards the stable or shade. It does not always follow that, because one eye is perfect, the other may not be tainted, although this may not be obvious at the moment.

Any disease in the eye, even from the slightest cold or inflammation, until it be completely cured, or until it has terminated in total blindness, stamps the animal as
UNSOUND.

All eyes predisposed to inflammation, although not actually affected by this complaint at the time of the warranty being drawn up, must be considered to stamp the horse as UNSOUND.

Where there is reason to suppose that all tendency to inflammation in these organs has ceased, whether from the animal's age or otherwise, if there are any marks of injury remaining—as is mostly the case—from the smallest cataract, not larger than a needle's point; or if there is the slightest dilatation of the pupil, the horse is UNSOUND.

In other words, a horse with either eye not actually perfect is, if not blind, unsound.

TOTAL BLINDNESS.

If the animal is totally blind, either with one or both eyes, then there is no danger accompanying his use beyond what can be easily calculated upon; and if he is capable of doing the same work as other horses of his class similarly afflicted, he may be warranted sound, ranking only as BLEMISHED.

THE MOUTH.

The age of the horse may be ascertained by examining the teeth and general appearance of the mouth. Taking it for granted that the reader will be acquainted with the peculiar structural marks, as reference can easily be made to plates on the subject, it only remains for me to state, that, by careful study and proper opportunity, one may learn to ascertain the age of the horse with tolerable accuracy, until the animal has turned his twentieth year. This is allowed by those who have had the opportunity and wish to ascertain the truth; but it is the interest of many to keep up the vulgar error that beyond the age of eight the horse's age cannot be calculated with any certainty. It is for this reason no one has a horse more than eight years old for sale!

CONTRACTED FEET.

Having already considered the general formation of the feet, we now take up the near fore one, to see whether it is in any way diseased, or whether there are symptoms of its having formerly been so.

To describe what should be the width of heel, and other peculiarities which form a perfect foot for each horse, would be indeed superfluous; such knowledge can be acquired only by study and practice. To point out the result of each defect when ascertained, so that the initiated may judge for themselves, is all that can be attempted. The thorough horesman is the only one who will appreciate more elaborate description. This assertion may perhaps appear over-confident; but, if blame attach to it, I hope those who have urged me on will lighten the burden. Thorough horsemen are comparatively few, but the incompetent are numerous. This work, it is to be hoped, will be the means of adding to the former by decreasing the latter.

It is a matter of dispute whether contraction of the foot renders the horse unsound or not. All will agree, where the climate is exceedingly hot and the horse goes sound, that this is a much better wearing foot, and more likely to keep free from lameness than the expanded soft hoof, which, from being wide, and predisposed in the sole to concavity, is, *par excellence*, pronounced sound; yet, in fact, while the narrow foot will stand equally well on wet, and on hard dry soil, on the latter the wide-spread flat foot will quickly give way on account of its proneness to injury from its softness.

As feet of this description are adapted only for the work such horses are required to perform in their native country, it may perhaps be right enough to call them sound, prior to receiving injury. It is for the buyer to judge whether or not they are adapted to the work he requires.

Still, why this weakly foot should be allowed to pass as sound, to the prejudice of the other, I have always been at a loss to know. The colt foaled with certain sized feet—the effect of the soil on which it was bred—although it has never been afflicted with lameness or disease of any kind, is said to have contracted feet, and is condemned as unsound, because it is imagined that its hoofs are narrower than Fancy's prescribed limits. "He is unsound," says one; "I am doubtful," says another, "whether, according to law, it is unsoundness; he seems to go very well at present. He might have been better had they been a little more open."

Why should this be? In the human being, not only in different nations, but in the same country, we see people with feet of various sizes, but they are all equally capable of walking and of common exertion. I never knew a fast runner or a great walker amongst bipeds who had an extremely large foot; on the contrary, the feet of pedestrians, properly so called, are mostly, if not of the moderate size, rather under it. "Yes," some will say, "but the human foot is not confined within a box of horn, capable of yielding but slightly." Most true; but nature fits the horn to the foot, and not the foot to the horn.

Horses, therefore, which have naturally small feet, but not so small as to cause them inconvenience, may without doubt be pronounced SOUND.

Should the various reasons stated in this and previous articles not be convincing, I may say that some of the best veterinary surgeons are of opinion that, where contraction is not attended by inconvenience to the animal, it ought not to be deemed an unsoundness, although in England it was legally decided as such many years ago. Some persons, however, pronounce it consistent with soundness, in spite of that decision. Professor Coleman once remarked, that he "cared not what had been decided, no jury, after such evidence as would now be brought into court, could decide in favor of so absurd a law."

The statutes respecting soundness have altered, and must continue to be altered, with the advance of time and improved veterinary knowledge. In Xenophon's time, when horses were not shod, the hardest hoof was considered the best and soundest, because it wore the longest, although it was upright and contracted. When instructing his soldiers how to choose horses, he describes these feet; but at the same time shows that he was aware of the evils of contraction brought on by disease, and he gives directions how it may be avoided. I shall here only add that extreme developments are as bad as malformations produced by disease or work.

ARTIFICIAL CONTRACTION.

Artificial contraction, which must most always be the result of disease, let the disease arise from bad management, bad shoeing, neglect, or whatever cause, may bring on inflammation. The horny sole will not contract upon its contents, until either in action, or in the stable, the horse ceases to rest some of his weight upon his heels. This resting contracts the internal foot; the heat contracts the horn to it, and alters the secretion, so that the horn either gets thicker and stronger, or so thin and tender as to become what is called a shelly hoof. This shows that naturally small and narrow feet are very different from artificial contraction, which can be cured only at the earliest stage of the disease. It may subsequently be sometimes relieved; but rarely, after an inflammation of a few weeks' standing, without a powerful remedy being applied, will there be so decided a cure effected as that the horse may be pronounced sound. If the contraction arose from a disease that had been cured, and the horse had been doing the work of horses of his class for six weeks without inconvenience or extraordinary care, then he is SOUND.

Lameness from contraction is preferable to the lameness consequent upon convex or pumice sole; the latter unfitting the horse for any but slow or moderate work.

In order that I may not be misunderstood in treating of artificial contraction, I should mention the exception to the rule, though I do not think that contraction which comes on gradually, and without an injury from a secondary natural cause, should be considered artificial. For instance, if from want of exercise the frog receives no pressure, the inside of the foot has less work to perform, and gradually shrinks or wastes, and the horn contracts. When this takes place gradually, without inflammation, and without causing lameness or inconvenience, the horse is SOUND.

CORNS.

Corns are an unsoundness. They are mostly on the inside heel, looking like a bruise or extravasated blood. They are more or less troublesome, according to the nature of the foot. In the low-heeled, thin, and brittle hoof, they are the worst and most troublesome; in the stronger hoof they are of less consequence; provided they are not soft corns or others of a serious character, and if the horse is a very superior animal, with good hoofs, going sound at the time, I should not reject him for my own use. Where the feet are otherwise good, with care and proper shoeing corns are soon cured. I would give the owner a short time to try and cure soft corns if the horse is otherwise sufficiently good. While a corn of any kind exists, the animal is UNSOUND.

Corns may be produced in so short a period, that, should you discover them immediately after purchase, you cannot return the horse, unless you can prove they existed prior to purchase.

If any reader of this, with feet most tender from bad corns, is wincing away in tight boots, he should be informed that there is no analogy between human corns and those of horses. The corn of the horse is a bruise similar to that caused by pinching up a piece of the skin, so as to leave the blood underneath, and which, previous to going away, assumes a black appearance. In the horse it is best to cut them out, and keep off the pressure till thoroughly recovered. Soft corns are the least common with horses, and are nearer akin to those of the human being. Animals afflicted in this way are UNSOUND.

SAND-CRACK.

This is a crack or fissure mostly situate in the inside quarter of the forefoot, beginning just below the coronet, between hair and hoof, and passing down towards the bottom of the foot. Attention should be paid to this the moment it is discovered, when the requisite treatment and two or three days' rest will enable the horse to go sound in his work. In a few days the bandages may be taken off. The horse will most probably remain free from sand-crack till about the same time in the following year, when, unless strict attention is paid to it, he may throw another. While the sand-crack is in existence the animal is UNSOUND.

When cured, he may be warranted as sound; but so long as the hoof is unsightly from the cure, it is a temporary BLEMISH.

Where any marks of the sand-crack still remain at the time of the warranty being taken, in order to render the seller more secure, it would be advisable to make this disease an exception.

The horse is not returnable if one or more of these fissures appear immediately after he becomes the property of the purchaser, because he is considered SOUND until they are formed. Dry, brittle, thin hoofs are the most subject to this disease, particularly where the action is high and the weather dry and sharp. Attention, with slight stimulants, will do much to strengthen these hoofs, and render them less subject to cracks. Should these cracks be neglected till sand and dirt find their way through the fissures, they become troublesome to heal, and are frequently the cause of permanent lameness.

FALSE QUARTER.

False quarter is a horizontal fissure in the inside quarter of the hoof. What has been said of sand-crack, applies in a great measure to this also. Till a cure is effected, the horse is UNSOUND.

Thin, weak hoofs are most subject to this, though treading with one foot upon the other will produce it in any feet. If the horse goes sound, and does not require particular treatment, he may be warranted as such. While any mark remains, it must be regarded as a blemish; but a blemish arising from a tread or accident on a good hoof will probably not appear.

THRUSHES.

Thrushes are situated in the frogs of the feet, rendering them ragged, and causing a fetid moisture to exude. Unless bad, and of old standing, they are not an unsoundness, and are readily cured in twenty-four hours; yet, as they constitute disease, and are deviations from the general rule of health, as implied in a warranty, and therefore open to dispute, I will endeavor to make you sufficiently acquainted with the subject to form an opinion for yourself, while giving the reasons for altering the rule.

The frogs are evidently intended to relieve the other portions of the foot from some of the weight of the horse. Besides the interior structure proving this, no stronger evidence of this use of the frogs can be adduced than that want of pressure will of itself produce thrushes, and that, when the foot is not too far gone (fleshy), gentle pressure greatly assists a cure. Stopping the feet improperly with dung, and allowing it to remain too long in the hoofs, will also produce them. The best preventive is pressure and cleanliness; for, when the frogs become a little ragged, loose sand, dirt, or small gravel insinuating itself into the place affected will ultimately cause a running and tenderness; and where thrushes are already formed, the greatest attention to cleanliness is required. Proper care and attention, however, will effect a cure in a few hours. Until the frogs become bad or troublesome, or the heels become tender or fleshy, they should not be considered an unsoundness; but when the original structure of the frog has become so altered as to be perpetually tender, rendering the horse liable to drop at every step, he is then unquestionably UNSOUND.

One reason why slight thrushes should be considered as not rendering the horse unsound is, that they are of little consequence, and easily cured; another reason is, that slight thrushes may be produced in twelve hours in the most healthy feet, that is, the frog may be made to produce a moist secretion in that time. No one, therefore, would be justified in giving a warranty were slight thrushes to be regarded as an unsoundness, as any one not pleased with his bargain would only have to produce them to be almost certain of success in an action against the seller. This is, therefore, allowed to be one of the deviations from the general rule—that any alteration of structure renders the horse unsound.

In cases where thrushes, however slight, are known to exist, the best and most secure way is, to warrant with this exception; as a litigious buyer might, if he did not like the horse in other respects, make this a plea for going into court to see whether he could not return his bargain, by making the existence of the disease a matter of importance. He would not gain his point, but the vexation and annoyance are better avoided.

Where thrushes are the result of severe contraction, this state of contraction is an UNSOUNDNESS.

To stop thrushes, when to a certain extent they are answering the purpose of setons, provokes more active inflammation. In the contracted foot, more especially, they should have their course, until they have arrived at a certain state. Then they should be stopped, in order to prevent worse diseases; they must, however, be dried gradually and with caution, and then the horse will most probably be SOUND.

BAR SHOES.

Wherever bar or round shoes are required, even though for a temporary purpose, the horse is unsound; for no disease is cured, whether sand-cracks, corns, thrushes, or whatever else it may be, so long as these are necessary.

LEATHER SOLES.

What has been said of bar shoes applies equally to leather soles also; for, where it is necessary to use these to enable the horse to perform his work safely or properly, as he requires extra care, the horse is not sound, let the cause be what it may.

No one will dispute that leather soles are of great good, enabling many a horse to work soundly that otherwise would be in great pain. They are much safer than bar shoes, where they answer the purpose, as the horse has a better hold of the ground. They are also less likely to produce thrushes or waste the frogs. For some feet, gutta-percha is better adapted than leather, on account of its being harder, and less yielding to sharp stones, particularly in wet weather. It is not so well, however, when the sole is not to be covered, except in the case of corns.

RING BONES.

Ring bones are situate above the hoof, being an ossification of the cartilages at the top of the coronet. If seen only in front of the pastern, whence the disease generally extends itself round the front of the hoof, in form of a ring, it is frequently of little consequence; but where it approaches the heels, the horse is fit for slow work only, the flexibility of the cartilage by its altered structure being lost. The cartilage is likely to be fractured by the ascent of the internal structure of the hoof on any extreme pressure being given to the frogs, either from accelerated speed or from treading on a stone. At slow work horses with these hoofs often last for years without accident, but when they do fracture the ossified part, they should be at once destroyed, or turned out till the fracture is united, in which case, though not sound, they often go apparently soundly, though they are ever afterwards liable to accidents. When this cure occurs they do not move in pain, but are still UNSOUND.

Where the disorganization is only in front of the pastern bone, and not in the way of any joint, or approaching the heels, all inflammation or disease has disappeared. The animal will suffer no inconvenience from quick work, and is therefore sound, but shows a BLEMISH.

CANKER.

Thrushes neglected will turn to canker. This disease in the hoof is easily detected, and is very troublesome to cure. A cankered horse is UNSOUND.

WINDGALLS.

Windgalls are situate at the bottom of the cannon bone on each side of the leg, just above the pastern joint, at the union of these two bones. They yield to pressure. They appear to the eye like small enlargements, and feel soft to the hand when it is passed over them. They are not an UNSOUNDNESS in themselves, unless, as in rare instances and very extreme cases, they occasion lameness.

They are a proof that the horse has done work, their size depending upon the age at which this work was done, and the neglect the horse was subjected to at the time.

Unless they are of the worst kind (the largest size), I never would reject a superior horse for windgalls. They are no inconvenience to him, and are not an unsoundness, becoming less and less as the work is decreased till they disappear altogether; they are never seen in very old and fairly-worked horses. With the exception of the above-mentioned case, horses having windgalls are SOUND.

BANDAGES.

Where the constant use of bandages is required to enable a horse to perform the ordinary work of horses of his class, he is UNSOUND.

Bandages are good things properly applied, and there is a great deal of humanity in their seasonable appropriation and right use. You should remember, however, that there may also be "too much of a good thing," and that by over doing the thing, or bandaging improperly, you defeat your own purpose.

Why is the hair on that horse's legs so curled? I can never see it without pitying the poor brute, and thinking of the purgatory he has endured, through the ignorance of the groom—ignorance it must be; kindness dictated the use of bandages, but kindness did not intend them to be a torture, which they became by being thus tight and stopping circulation. As errors arising from good nature are the easiest cured; once show that these errors cause the pain which should be prevented, and they are not likely to occur again. When bandages are used, they should never be drawn tightly round the horse's legs, for in that case they weaken instead of strengthen, and cause the hair to curl. Put bandages lightly and easily round the leg; a very little keeps them up, and should they come down a hundred times, it is better than that the horse should be tortured once. There are very few who will not, in a trifling number of applications, acquire the habit of fitting them so easily that they are a great comfort and very serviceable to the legs under many circumstances, and will not curl the hair or leave unsightly marks; nor will they, when thus properly put on, punish the horse, or slip down.

SPLENTS.

Splents are hard bony lumps at the inside of the leg, towards the back of the cannon bone, anywhere below the knee and above the pastern joints, but mostly midway between the joints named, in which situation they are of the least consequence.

They are occasioned by breaking the colt too young, by blows from the fork to make him lift his legs off the straw when his bed is being made, kicks from the groom, blows from each other, or received in leaping, from strains, from being over-weighted, and from cutting the inside heel too low, whereby too much weight is thrown upon the sesamoid bone, which is the small bone at the back of the leg or cannon bone, and between it and the tendon.

While forming, they frequently occasion great lameness, on account of the inflammation going on while nature is uniting the small bone (sesamoid) behind to the cannon (or large bone of the leg), that they may strengthen one another. Generally splents are only found on the legs of young horses; for, although nature does not again disunite the bones, she absorbs those lumps which are conspicuous in the young horse.

After this union, it is presumed that the horse is not as springy as before; I must say, however, I never discovered any difference in elasticity. But, as they do not inconvenience him after they are completely formed, and all inflammation has ceased, so that he goes free from pain (and as it is allowed that his legs are stronger and less liable than formerly to injury) it is a blemish of the least consequence only, and the animal can be warranted as SOUND.

As the horse gets older, these excrescences disappear, although the union of the bones is asfirm as ever.

SPEEDY CUT.

Speedy cut is seen on the inside, and rather on the hind edge and lower corner, of the knee. Sometimes the bone is enlarged without any bald place to assist in detecting the habit, at others the skin only is cut; sometimes both. Like other enlargements, it may increase from an almost imperceptible size and little inconvenience, to a size both conspicuous and unsightly, as well as dangerous.

Speedy cut is occasioned by the horse twisting his legs in action, so as to strike the shoe or foot of the one leg against the knee of the other. It is done when the horse is going faster, or being driven more up to the bit, at the same time stepping higher, than he is capable of doing with propriety.

Horses given to this action are mostly good-couraged, and a thorough horseman who knows how to make them step without touching, at the same time bringing out their good qualities, sometimes obtains a pleasant horse quite cheaply.

To others than good horsemen, such animals are very dangerous—dear at a gift. Boots are a little safeguard. Down hill is their worst chance, and the attempt at holding them up, except by the thorough horseman, too often brings them down.

Reject them if you value your limbs and neck, although they are allowed to be SOUND; and properly so, where they are capable of going at the usual pace without inconvenience, performing the usual work of horses of their class (not speedy cutters) with ordinary usage, without the necessity of boots or more than ordinary care. But where, as is frequently the case, the horse cannot travel usual distances at the ordinary pace, with the common rate of horsemen, without seriously cutting and otherwise endangering himself, there ought to be a difference; I myself do not believe that he is SOUND. I would recommend the seller, where there is the least tendency to this defect, always to except speedy cutting in his receipt; otherwise, he is likely to get into a dilemma. The door is open for dispute. Where is the man who is not a horseman in his own estimation? Who is there among our acquaintances that, if he is not a whip or horseman of the first water, is not considerably above the average? Do you know any one so modest as to allow that he belongs to the second-class? On the contrary, have you not found that, however ignorant they may have been before they had a horse, with their first they have become miraculously invested with all the abilities of Phaeton? Well, then, they have only to state their case to a lawyer, when he replies that it is a capital plea for an action; but actions are expensive and vexatious, and as all the evils above enumerated are to be avoided by a little caution, will it not be better to use it?

HOCKS.

The hocks are an important part of the horse; his speed, strength, and capability to perform certain kinds of work depending almost entirely, if not altogether, upon these joints.

The blood horse cannot be a racer without sufficient leverage in the hocks to give him both speed and strength.

The hunter must be but a poor leaper without a certain perfection here; and then, in proportion to this desirable state, all other things combining, so will he vary from the best to the worst horse of his description.

The parade or ménage horse, in order to be good and capable of continuing even for a few minutes at the height of parade action, must have these parts quite as strong as any other description of horse.

The military horse, again, although not having them called into such violent exertion, or so frequently as the three kinds above-mentioned, yet from being set a great deal upon his haunches, and having to halt suddenly, and being heavily weighted, requires much strength here.

This is one of the principal reasons why these horses are usually found such good workers.

Ladies' horses, perhaps have their hocks most tried in proportion to the weight they carry, from their continually cantering. This pace is most calculated to try these joints, from the long exertion required in the one pace. If proper horses for ladies to ride, they are "well upon their haunches," and stop as well as the charger, with their hind legs well under them.

In fact, no horse can be either easy, safe, or satisfactory to ride, that does not take a large proportion of his burden on his hind legs.

The hackney has some relief by change from one pace to the other. But to be superior, he must take the weight on his hind legs; this enables him to go in a corky, light, and springy manner,—no shaking. You will hear this perfection thus described: "He goes as light as a cork," "would not break an egg." Horses thus trained cannot shake you; neither can they fall or stumble.

The harness horse has neither to canter nor leap, neither has he weight upon his back. Here you have to consider the speed required, and the weight he has to draw, with the style of action you desire; whether you will be satisfied with merely being moved along, or whether you wish to make a dash; how much of a pace, of action, or of grandeur, you require or are willing to sacrifice.

CURBS.

Curbs are hard bony enlargements at the back and on the lower part of the hock. They may be of such little consequence as to be called only enlargements on the seat of curb, or large enough to be curbs. While forming, the horse is sure to be lame. Either they are a proof that the hocks are ill-formed (weak), or are the result of mismanagement, over-work, strains, or blows. Ignorant breakers are the principal originators of curbs. Kicking in harness, or against the stalls, or any hard substance, will produce them on the best-formed hocks. When they have assumed a decided form, and have become hard bony substances, and all inflammation has left, if the horse goes sound, do not reject him, should he suit in all other respects.

Whether a curbed horse is sound or unsound is a matter of dispute. There are partisans on both sides, but I think the majority agree with me in opinion that, where he is capable of doing all the work required of horses of his class, as well with the curbs as without them, he is
SOUND.

If the curbs are large enough to be distinctly seen, or are disfigured by treatment or otherwise, they are
BLEMISHES.

To save trouble and expense, the best way, where there is the slightest enlargement, or the least doubtful quality, is to make an exception in the warranty. (See copy of receipt, with warranty, on a subsequent page.) Where the hocks are naturally ill-formed and weak, the horse is
UNSOUND.

While forming, the horse being lame, it is almost useless to mention that he is indisputably UNSOUND.

It is now to be hoped that from all I have said you will see that it is your fault if, from this cause, you lose a good horse from fastidious fear, or take a useless one screened by customary subterfuge.

SPAVINS.

Spavins are enlargements on the inside, and rather toward the front of the hock; they are produced in the same manner as curbs.

If completely formed and low down, quite away from the joint, and rather behind, and the horse goes sound, having hocks otherwise perfect, do not reject him.

These also occasion difference of opinion. You never find a hunter that has done any work, without his having either the seat of curb or that of spavin enlarged. He is, nevertheless, sound, and capable of doing work better than the younger ones. Both diseases are brought on by the same causes. Perhaps, of the two, the spavin is more the result of severe work, when there is generally some little stiffness. Too often the groom treats the wrong places; or if he does treat the right ones, yet the evil is only deferred, for if the horse is continued at severe work, the spavins will form and re-form. Proper treatment may prevent their being of the larger size, and may lessen the evil. When they have formed, and the horse does his work like the rest of the old ones who have gone through the same process, the groom commends himself for the result, and the owner congratulates himself upon the improved constitution (strength) of the horse.

Taking all parts of the hocks into consideration, if they are affected by what is termed enlargement on the seat of spavin, the disease being determined, and not likely to increase, I need hardly say that, if the horse goes sound, he is, according to common sense, SOUND.

The law, however, being unsettled, cases having been decided both ways, the best way is, as in the case of curb and other diseases, to except spavins in the warranty.

Here it may be as well to state the opinion of a well-known sportsman and horseman, not on account of its being an exclusive opinion of his own, but as the opinion of most practical men of his class. He states, that there are no hunters without curbs or spavins, or both, and that they are SOUND.

Horses with enlarged hocks, going sound, are sold almost every day, with a warranty, without the least suspicion being entertained of their being wrong. All those acquainted with hunting establishments and the hocks of horses must be aware that there does not seem to arise any inconvenience from the practice. Why then should not this custom become a law? At all horse repositories, you will see horses with these enlargements, but going SOUND, sold with a warranty, the buyer rarely discovering that there ever was the least flaw.

CAPPED HOCKS.

Capped hocks are the result of blows, not unfrequently from kicking, or rubbing against sharp corners of the stall-post. Stone or fluted iron pillars at the back end of the stalls are the most frequent cause. They are unsightly, but they in no way inconvenience the animal, unless suppuration takes place, when they heal soon, and the swelling disappears. While this suppuration is going on, and the wound is unhealed, as there is a disease in progress, the horse is UNSOUND.

Although in itself simple, there is no telling with certainty what will be the result: but when the horse is cured, he is SOUND.

Where these is no appearance of suppuration taking place, he is SOUND.

Where capped hocks, from their size, become a disfigurement to the horse, a suspicious sign on harness horses, they must be recorded as a BLEMISH.

GROGGY.

Horses that are what is usually termed groggy do not nod, or, rather, bow their heads, on account of being equally lame with both forefeet. Their ears are placed backwards when in action, and there is a peculiarity about their stepping, as if from anxiety to retain their feet upon the ground each time they touched it. There is also a peculiarity in the working of the shoulder-blades, and, in spite of their mostly going well upon their haunches to relieve their forefeet, they are very shaky and unpleasant, more especially when put into the canter. Some consider them easy in the trot. They ought, however, to be used only in harness, or where there is no weight on the back: they are UNSOUND.

LAME.

Horses when more tender in one foot than the other—presuming it is the forefoot or leg—droop the head when they step upon the unsound foot, and raise it when stepping on the sound one; they also step "longer" with the lame one than the sound one, and keep it a shorter time on the ground. You may hear the lame foot touch the ground lighter than the sound one with its hard, firm, short step. Lameness is the language of pain, expressing no more than the animal really feels; it tells the plain and honest truth, with the greatest simplicity. Is not this the strongest appeal to our sympathies? Ought we not to attend to their dictates, and do all we can to relieve their sufferings?

A little care at the proper period will often prevent a lameness becoming permanent. Slight attention will relieve the pain of the incurable.

Many horses, which go lame with weight upon their backs, will go sound in single harness, because the weight is lessened; and often, where lame here, will go sound in double, because there is no weight at all.

Instead of riding a lame horse, try single or double harness. There are some who can perform slow work without pain, even on the road, when they are no longer fit for fast work; and even when the road is too hard, they may work about a farm. I need hardly add that there is great cruelty in keeping horses to any fast work when lame in it, and that frequently at slow work, particularly on soft ground, they will become sound if kept a sufficient time employed upon it. From the preceding observations, you will see the propriety of having the horse ridden prior to purchase.

One fallacy I must here point out, as it is often practised by persons who would not be guilty of cruelty, if they imagined they were perpetrating it; and many others may be deterred by the money consideration: it is the mistake of keeping horses at work when they are lame, thinking that they will work sound. It must be remembered that all lameness, with rare exceptions, is curable (if proper remedies are resorted to) with perfect rest at the commencement of the disease. But if lameness continues without remedy beyond six weeks, some disorganization will take place. The diseases of horses are rapid in their progress and quickly come to a definite termination; and though, after neglect, the disease may be mitigated, the horse can never be restored to PERFECT SOUNDNESS, but will most probably be a cripple and in pain to the end of his days. In the earliest stages of the disease, too, the injured part is more easily discovered. This is more than half the cure.

Nor is the veterinarian to be blamed for not being too confident as to the immediate seat of disease. The horse cannot point to an affected part and say, "There I feel the pain;" but together, horse and doctor will soon understand enough of each other to hit upon the spot and work right.

When lame behind, horses carry their heads high, go with a catch of the hind leg, and roll the hips. Every species of lameness and tenderness is an UNSOUNDNESS.

RHEUMATISM.

Rheumatism can be discovered only when the horse is lame, and, consequently, unsound; but should you be able to prove that the horse was afflicted with rheumatism within a reasonable time of purchase, and that he was subject to that disease before you purchased him,— even though he was going sound at the time of purchase, —if he was warranted, he is returnable. This is a disease generally brought on horses by carelessness and the supposition that they are never afflicted by it. Horses should not be exposed to draughts, particularly in the stable, the flooring of which, more especially the straw, should be dry for them to lie upon. As horses are exposed to damp and cold out of doors, people imagine it matters not what condition the stable may be in, thinking only that, if foul, it may spoil their coats. Out of doors and at liberty horses are not exposed to draughts; whenever they can they will get out of them; and when unpleasantly cold, will move about and warm themselves. This they have not room to do in the stable. Do they ever lie down in the wet out of doors? They choose the driest spot they can find; and when cold, they will either roll and get an extra layer of dirt as a covering, or otherwise exercise themselves.

For this disease it is usual to treat in the vicinity of the round bone. Therefore, when you see marks of blistering, setons, or firing on this part, even though the horse at the time of examination goes free from lameness, you have reason to apprehend occasional inconvenience from the temporary lameness occasioned by this complaint; and, while subject to the return at intervals, or where it is a determined complaint of the horse, the animal is UNSOUND.

Where the cure has been effected some time and no relapse had occurred, as it is clear that the malady has not become a constitutional complaint of the horse, then it may be considered that a permanent cure has been effected, and the animal be warranted as   SOUND.

THOROUGH PINS.

There are few horses who have done any work without acquiring thorough pins. They are a windgall in the hock. Unless they cause inconvenience, which is rarely the case, the horse is   SOUND.

BLOOD SPAVIN.

Blood spavin is the enlargement of the thigh vein, where it passes over the inside of the hock. It is known by giving way and disappearing in a great degree upon pressure being applied below it; but it returns as soon as the pressure is removed. Blood spavins never produce lameness, and are of rare occurrence. Severe strains, bruises, or other local injuries are the cause. Some will not admit that the disease is an unsoundness, while others maintain that it is. Be it which it may, in those cases where it proves of no consequence, it can only be fastidiousness to refuse the horse; therefore, no reasonable person will object to this being excepted from the warranty.

Blood spavins may be produced in an instant. One step or slip is sufficient; therefore, admitting it is an unsoundness, and you discovered one, half an hour after purchase, you could not return the horse, unless you could prove he had had it prior to purchase.

This may appear strange at first sight; but when you reflect that, even though you may not have moved the horse one yard, a slip in the stall, a blow, or getting up in a hurry, may produce them, you must see that it is no more than just that the seller's responsibility should end with delivery; in at least so far that it becomes your duty after acceptance, should the defect appear, to prove that the disease or tendency thereto existed prior to delivery or date of warranty.

BOG SPAVIN.

Bog spavin is a windgall on the inside front of the hock joint. After it is once formed, and all heat and inflammation are gone, it is rarely of any consequence.

Where it does not interfere with the horse's action, and he has done the ordinary work of horses of his class for the required time since it formed, without extra rest, or inconvenience, then is he SOUND.

STRING HALT.

This disease may be at once detected by the awkward catch of the leg affected, the action of this leg being much higher than the others, and drawn up by a jerk. It is seldom seen in both hind legs. The collapse of the muscle, which is by some persons supposed to be the cause of this peculiar action, is occasioned by the interior of the muscle having been formed into a kind of cyst or bag by an abscess which, having discharged the pus, leaves the interior of the muscle open. It is frequently supposed to arise from inflammation of the nerve; while others say it is an excess of energy without disease; if the latter is the case, and the horse experiences no pain, or weakness, or anything to prevent it from working as well as ever, he is SOUND.

This defect should, however, always be mentioned by the vendor.

But supposing others to be right who conjecture that

it is occasioned by an inflamed nerve, then it must be UNSOUND.

I should, therefore, advise the warranty to have this disease excepted.

LOW HIP.

One hip being lower than the other is occasioned by a blow having knocked the lower one out of its place. It is, in fact, a fracture, and the broken part being unreplaceable, is drawn down by the muscles and unites below its original place. When the horse ceases to go lame, as he usually soon does, he is sound; it must, nevertheless, be recorded in the warranty as a BLEMISH.

OTHER DISEASES OF JOINTS.

With the other joints all difficulty is soon removed, as they show their diseases by lameness, and when well they are SOUND.

If any enlargement or scar remains, it is a BLEMISH.

GREASE.

Grease is a disease seldom seen in well-managed stables. It is a proof of neglect. If recent, it is easily cured, and is, therefore, of little consequence. Till cured, the horse is UNSOUND.

Afterwards, SOUND.

CRACKED HEELS.

When of recent occurrence, cracked heels are of less consequence than grease. Till cured, the animal is UNSOUND.

Afterwards, SOUND.

SWOLLEN LEGS.

When swollen legs proceed from dropsy, or farcy, or are of long standing, and therefore a sign of general debility, they are difficult of cure, and the horse is mostly useless, except for slow work, and therefore
UNSOUND.

In the milder forms, where the swelling arises either from too much fatigue, or from want of medicine, whether tonics, depletants, or exercise, until cured the horse is UNSOUND.

When the swelling is permanently removed SOUND.

STARING COAT.

Where the horse's coat is harsh, dry, and staring, you may at once make up your mind that he is
UNSOUND.

If he has not an active disease, he has a chronic one. Roarers, whistlers, those with old coughs and broken wind and subject to megrims, old crib biters, wind-suckers, etc., etc., all have their coats more or less affected.

WENS.

A wen situate about the upper part of the windpipe, or upon any main vein or artery, where it is likely to be of consequence, is an UNSOUNDNESS.

But if wens occur on other parts, as on the top of the hock, termed cap hock, on the elbow, or on any other place where they are of little consequence, and could be removed without danger if they should become an inconvenience, but at present appear at a fixed and determined size and form, then is the horse SOUND.

CUTTING.

Should there be any places on the inside of the pastern joint which have at some period had the hair knocked off by the foot of the opposite leg, which you may know to be the fact by the little bald places that remain ever after, you must examine the action and present condition of the horse, so as to ascertain whether it was weakness, poverty, being over-worked, or worked too young, bad horsemanship, or a natural defect in the action of the horse, that induced cutting.

This last ought to be an UNSOUNDNESS, according to the rule laid down, and is so, where the malformation is so serious as to render the horse naturally incapable of doing the work of horses of his class, unless, whatever his breed, he is to be numbered with the slow-draught horses; in that case he is inefficient, not being capable of the ordinary work of horses of his class.

When a horse uses his legs so awkwardly that on the least exertion he must cut them—whether the peculiar gait of the animal has been acquired by bad management, or from usage in the breaking, or from malformation—my opinion is that he is UNSOUND.

The law should be governed by common sense, and a jury, I feel confident, would be of the same opinion; for in this latter case it is only by extreme care and not tiring the horse that you can keep his legs from becoming raw. While the legs are in that state any horse is UNSOUND.

It requires care to keep him from falling. Cuts prevent his doing the work of horses of his class with ordinary care, and this renders him doubly dangerous, as horsemen will not be troubled with so unsatisfactory an animal.

Where the horse has been cut through over-fatigue or poverty, and has recovered from the weakness consequent thereon, requiring no more care than other horses, the wounds being healed, he is SOUND.

RAT TAIL.

Rat tail is indiscriminately employed to describe the tail of the horse when it is either quite free from hair or partially so. It does not prevent the horse in any way from being SOUND.

Although unsightly, it is not a blemish that will enable the purchaser to return the horse, as it is impossible not to notice so glaring a disfigurement. When it is covered by false hair, or any other fraud is practised in order to hide it, the offence is punishable.

This is considered by some a sign of a good horse. What the loss of the hair off the tail has to do with the qualities of the animal we do not pretend to fathom; perhaps the notion has arisen from the naked stump giving an appearance of width to its quarters. The itching occasioned by disease sometimes causes both good and bad horses to become minus their tail-hair.

Keeping the tail well and frequently washed with soft soap will always reproduce the hair in the earlier stages, and not unfrequently in cases of long standing.

UNNERVING.

Horses having had the operation of neurotomy (popularly called unnerving) performed upon them go free from lameness, with action more or less high, their step being hard and heavy; the height of action and degree of hardness of tread depend on the way the operation is performed and the place operated upon. To discover whether the high operation has been performed, that is, depriving of feeling every portion of the leg and foot below the marks described, pass the hand along the back sinew; if the horse catches up the leg sharply, this ought to excite your suspicion. If you find one or two little knobs or lumps, you have still stronger reason for suspicion; but if it is, on these scars being pressed, that he lifts his legs suddenly, depend upon it that he has been unnerved there, and that therefore they will never wear any great length of time,—most probably not three months. Should the symptoms just described present themselves on feeling along the back of the pastern, between the junction of the cannon-bone and the pastern, and the foot, the operation of neurotomy has been performed at that place. In the latter case, the unnerving has been performed on the back of the pastern-joint, the foot being deprived of feeling at the hinder portion only. The horse is capable of showing any injury the other portions of the foot receive,—as pricks from the blacksmith, bruises from stones, etc. He therefore stands a better chance of having his ailments attended to before it is too late. How long they will work, apparently sound, after the operation, is altogether a lottery; in some instances, with the lower operation, the horse works free from pain for many years; therefore, in some cases of lameness, it is an act of humanity to have the horse unnerved, as it may save him many years of suffering, and enable him to retain his serviceableness to the last. But it is seldom worth any one's while to buy under such risk, particularly if recently performed; for, should the navicular disease be present, although, since the operation, the animal has been free from lameness, a fracture of the union of the navicular and coffin bones at the minute joint which they form within the horny hoof will be the result, and speedy death from mortification will most probably follow.

COURAGE.

That the horse does not give way readily to pain, there are numerous instances on record. He rushes on the sword when he feels the point pierce his bosom. However fatigued or ill he may be, on he plods his weary way till death kindly relieves him. What other animal does this? Man himself sometimes dies from over-exertion, but seldom while in the act. The dog—the faithful companion who never forsakes his master—when over-fatigued will lie down on the wayside, leaving his friend to proceed alone; no entreaty can urge him unto death. Not so the poor, ill-requited, over-worked, abused horse; neither pain nor privation checks his services, as the following authenticated anecdote, as well as many other instances which must rush upon the memory of every horseman, or of any one who reads a newspaper, serves to illustrate; besides, the circumstance serves to show the effect of the operation, described in the preceding article on unnerving when performed upon an improper subject, and the indomitable spirit just referred to. Hearing the following tale related as having occurred in Scotland, I took some pains, when travelling through that country, to ascertain the particulars.

The mare which is the subject of this story belonged to a Mr. Miens, a large coach proprietor in Glasgow. After some trouble I saw him, when he told me the mare I referred to was a chestnut, that she ran a stage between Carlisle and Glasgow as leader, that she had been unnerved—the high operation—and that the disease for which she was operated upon was the navicular. One dark night, about three or four months after the operation, the coachman felt her drop, but she recovered herself, and ran to the end of the stage. She was then discovered to be very lame, and, upon examination in the stable, it was found that the whole of the foot was off, and that she must consequently have run some distance on the stump of the leg bone. The next morning the foot was discovered at a distance of not less than two miles from the inn she arrived at, and, from other marks upon the road, it was clear that the poor beast must have come at least that distance on the raw and dislocated stump.

I have entered more fully into this operation than into any other, as I have often found it difficult to make people understand how it is that the horse is not sound or cured by that operation which takes away the lameness.

Although the lower portion of the limb is never restored to its natural quick sensibility, if the horse works free from pain for from two or three years, there is every probability that he will continue to do so, the nerve being united, the horse can perform all the work of horses of his class; yet, until we have better data to go upon as to the mischief resulting from injuries in consequence of this muffled or deadened sensation, he must still be pronounced UNSOUND.

CHINKED BACK.

Chinked back, which is a slight dislocation or injury of the vertebræ or of the spinal cord running through them, is caused by the horse being pulled up suddenly by an unskillful horseman, or being over-weighted. The misfortune occurs in a moment, where the horse is stopped on the instant, unless his legs are properly placed at the precise time; it is therefore dangerous for any but an accomplished horseman to attempt it, and more especially from the circumstance that the horse is not a returnable purchase if you discover this defect a few minutes after purchase, unless you can prove that the injury existed prior to his becoming your property. When the horse drops at the pastern joint of the hind legs while being ridden, you have reason to apprehend this defect, particularly where you find that the front of the hind pastern joint has been cut or injured at any time, or that the horse grunts on being backed, or winces on being pressed on the affected part. UNSOUND.

Where the injury is slight, chinked-back horses frequently carry light weights very well, but are best in harness, more particularly in double harness. How long they may keep usable depends on the management of those who use them, and upon their proper adaptation to their work. UNSOUND.

BROKEN BACK.

The name sufficiently explains this injury. It is known by an aggravation of all the symptoms mentioned in chinked-back, added to which broken-backed horses cannot kick. They may work a little as leaders in carts, or do other slow work. At all events, when you are a buyer, consider them useless and UNSOUND.

DROPPING BEHIND.

Dropping behind, or knuckling with the pastern joint or joints, may be produced by chinked or broken back. (See both these articles.) In either of these cases the horse is UNSOUND.

Where, as is frequently the case, it is merely occasioned by a pressure upon the kidneys from want of medicine, until the physic, when applied, has ceased to affect him, the horse is UNSOUND.

When the medicine has worked off, if he no longer drops, he is SOUND.

Sometimes an awkward-fitting saddle will occasion him to drop as above described. Here you have only to remove the cause, when it is hardly necessary to add that the horse is SOUND.

STUMBLING.

In the well-formed horse, stumbling is an impossibility, unless he is leg-weary, the shoes do not fit properly, or the saddle hurts him; mind not what either the saddler or groom says, but depend upon it that the saddle does hurt him, if, upon examination, you find that the shoes do not hurt. I have seen too many instances of their mistakes to care what they say, and am convinced that very few really know when a saddle does fit. I have bought many horses that had got into disgrace for this fault, but they have never stumbled after they came into my possession. The secret was, I took care to have a saddle that fitted both the horse and my own ideas. (See article on Broken Knees.) Persevere in using a misfitting saddle, and the horse will fall.

LAMENESS.

Should your horse go lame behind when mounted, and not at other times, as this most probably is caused by the saddle pressing on the backbone, try another saddle. The same remark applies to his going lame before, under similar circumstances, except that in this case the saddle hurts the foreparts.

If, when the saddle is changed, he goes free from lameness, the animal may be considered SOUND.

DROPPING BEFORE.

Dropping before, or knuckling with the pastern joint of the forefoot, if not occasioned by tender feet or weakness, but arising solely from youth or carelessness, does not affect the horse's soundness.

The exceptions are treated under their respective heads; in these cases horses are UNSOUND.

Dropping before may be occasioned by treading on a stone, by a misfitting saddle, or by accidents of any kind. In either of the last-mentioned cases, the horse is
            Sound.

See the preceding three articles.

If the dropping-before arises from malformation or tender feet, the horse is   Unsound.

FLESHY HEEL.

Fleshy heel is an abnormal structure of the frog, wherein the sensitive part of the foot becomes too much exposed, the horse thereby being more or less tender according to the progress of the disease, and therefore
            Unsound.

CUNNING LAMENESS.

In those cases in which horses are said to sham lameness, that is, appearing sound at one time and unsound at another, there is invariably something wrong; it is not a case of shamming, but of painful reality. (See the article on "Unnerving.") In such cases a reason can always be found, either in a slight touch of rheumatism, paralysis, or non-adjustment or misfit of the saddle.

To illustrate these facts, I will mention one out of the many cases that have come under my notice.

A friend of mine had a delightful little mare, remarkable for her height in the withers, named "Brunette." This mare I was requested to examine with a view towards discovering the *rationale* of her continually stumbling in a very serious manner, and at uncertain and unexpected times.

She was certain, if she made one initiatory stumble, to continue stumbling all day; contrariwise, if she did not stumble soon after starting, she might be trusted to do her day's work throughout, without stumbling.

Upon examining her as to form, etc., I concluded that the cause of this misbehavior must be in some fault in her tackle, and I therefore inquired whether she always wore the same saddle. I was told that she wore various saddles, which were shown to me; I therefore selected and marked one for her use, and very shortly afterwards she ceased stumbling.

Her groom had always considered this habit to be a mischievous trick on her part, induced by her recollecting having been brought home by her master in consequence of the stumbling; and he told me that if she had been well punished in the first instance, she would have had the trick flogged out of her, and would have given no subsequent trouble. I myself believe that had such a course been adopted, the mare would have had her knees broken, and that fistula would soon have been developed upon her withers.

As it now appeared that, though she had ceased to stumble or go lame when ridden with an ordinary saddle, she invariably went lame when ridden by a lady. I was asked whether I could account for this peculiarity otherwise than by cunning. Again I referred the evil to the saddle; and, upon inquiry, I found that the owner had hitherto been unable to procure a side-saddle of such a make as not to raw the back of the mare when used by a lady for an hour or two at a time, making it necessary, therefore, that the next day should be, so to speak, wasted in paying attention to the abrasion thus produced. I also ascertained that the stuffing of the side-saddle had been altered and shifted every time she went out—about three times a week. I sent for the saddler and showed him what was wanting; but he either could not, or would not understand me; and although he had had the saddle several times under his hands, he had not been able to alter it, so as to make it fit for more than one or two day's work. Happening to be present on the last occasion on which he brought back the saddle, and knowing how repeatedly he had failed to make it fit, I made some remarks which excited his anger, and he declared that no one could succeed better than he had done, and defied any one to make a lady's saddle that would not hurt the mare. I therefore altered the saddle myself, and successfully; for, during several subsequent years in which my friend kept and used the mare, she never went lame, never had a sore back, and never made one single stumble.

How often has it fallen to my lot to see good horses sacrificed needlessly, through the use of insufficient or inappropriate tackle, and apparently becoming lame and weakened!

BEARING-REIN.

Among the many advantages of dispensing with the bearing-rein, not the least is that of doing away with the nut which fastens the hook in the saddle, as this not uncommonly hurts the horse's back, producing, if not broken knees and fistula, at least a troublesome sore on the withers.

Whether such a result be the smallest pimple or the largest wen, the merest abrasion or the foulest ulcer, the horse is, in any case UNSOUND.

When the sore is healed, and the horse is restored to perfect usefulness, he is again SOUND.

When the saddle hurts the horse so much as to cause him to go lame, or to fall upon his knees, and no sore is visible on the removal of the saddle, he is SOUND.

But, should there be any wound caused by the saddle, the animal is, until cured, UNSOUND.

Under no circumstances should the bearing-rein be tight. When it is too tight it prevents the animal from throwing the necessary weight upon the collar, disturbs the circulation to the head, and causes apoplexy, megrims, and other evils. But in double harness the bearing-rein should be sufficiently tight to prevent the horses from catching their bits in the pole-piece, though this prevention is sometimes attempted by removing the lower bar from the bit. What is thereby avoided, however, at the bottom of the bit, frequently occurs to an equal extent by the catching of the cheek of the bit in the other horse's head-gear.

I have dwelt thus far upon the injuries arising from a misfitting saddle, as they cause great annoyance and pain to the horse, as well as inconvenience to the owner, and are easily rectified by any one who will take the trouble to look in the right direction for the cause; especially as the same remarks apply to all parts of misfitting trapping, such as saddles, bridles, harness, rollers, head-stalls, etc. For in this case, what is true of one part applies to all the horse's furniture, when even the slightest injury is caused to him.

A misfitting bridle or winker may, and often does, produce blindness or severe shying; yet this, like many other simple things, has been often overlooked or misapprehended, from a natural proneness to forget that "great events from little causes spring."

Thus, in "Brunette's" case, before named, I proved that the fault lay in the saddle. Some persons attributed her habit of stumbling to cunning; others, of a more scientific turn of mind, stated it, variously, to be partial paralysis; the remains of an old strain only felt by the mare when carrying a one-sided weight; or the result of an old strain, which, owing to the almost imperceptible changes in the atmosphere, affecting, as such changes do, the constitutions of all animals, affected her more at one time than at another.

True it is that the weather and atmosphere exercise

considerable influence on the health and spirits of horses; it is, nevertheless, unnecessary to seek out remote and unaccountable causes, until we have examined the more matter-of-fact ones which are within our reach.

SINEWS.

When the sinews at the back of the fore legs become thickened, between the knee and the pastern joint, as there is always more or less weakness or irritability resulting from old strains, the horse is UNSOUND.

When the sinews of the hind leg, between the hock and the pastern, become thickened, even if this thickening vanishes when the horse takes exercise, he must be held to be UNSOUND.

If, on the contrary, such thickening be the result of a blow, appears callous, does not occasion inconvenience, and does not decrease when the horse is at exercise, the horse must, in that respect, be esteemed SOUND.

Great care must, in such cases, be taken that he do not kick when in harness.

BROKEN WIND.

The disease, broken wind, is easily recognized by the horse's peculiar suppressed cough when at exercise, after a hearty meal, or upon being changed from one kind of atmosphere to another,—as, for instance, from the stable air to a cold and foggy atmosphere, or *vice versa.*

If you observe a horse thus afflicted, when he is quiet, you may notice that the flank appears to distend and contract twice while the ribs rise once.

Immediately after brisk exercise this labored breath is still more apparent; the nostrils being more or less distended, and a peculiar seam or wrinkle between them being perceptible, whereas in horses of "good wind" no such mark can be found.

Broken-winded horses are UNSOUND.

ROARING.

Horses afflicted with the disease named roaring make, when galloping or trotting, a peculiar noise, the nature of which is sufficiently indicated by its name. Such horses, upon being suddenly agitated, checked, or pulled up short, make more or less of this noise, according to the progress the disease has made. Roaring is a chronic disease of the windpipe, or perhaps, more correctly, the remains of such a disease; but when it is not acute or serious, the horse does not appear to suffer much inconvenience from it in its earlier stages, although the noise caused by it is very unpleasant; if the horse is put to fast work, the noise will increase, till it at last becomes most distressing to both horse and user.

The roarer's coat usually indicates a departure from robust health, however fat the horse may be.

Such a horse is adapted to slow work only, and is
 UNSOUND.

GRUNTING.

Although grunting, which is produced in the horse by his being suddenly agitated by the use of spur or whip, or by his being pulled up hastily, is not unlike roaring, yet as he does not make the former sound on any other occasion, I believe the two affections, roaring and grunting, to be quite distinct.

The coat of the grunter does not imply disease.

I myself have never known, nor have I ever met any one who has known, this complaint to change into roaring; yet, as many persons think it probable that it might do so, and that it may be the remains of some disease, the horse is considered to be UNSOUND.

My opinion is that the noise proceeds from nervousness, and not from any disease; and that as it does not hinder the animal from performing the labor due from one of his class, the horse is SOUND.

However, as opinions differ upon this subject, the safest course is to bar even grunting in a warranty for soundness.

WHISTLING.

The presence of whistling is easily ascertained by a sharp gallop, which will quickly cause, if it be present, the wheezing or whistling noise. This malady may or may not be curable. When it is only attendant upon another disease, the whistling will vanish with the disease: thus, for instance, it frequently accompanies a cold, but, on the cold being cured, vanishes and is not heard again. Where it assumes a chronic form, as it frequently does when produced by water on the chest, by inflammation of the lungs, or by injury to the windpipe, it is incurable.

As the cold is, *per se*, an unsoundness, whistling is, of course, in this, its least aggravated form, an

UNSOUNDNESS.

When a good and serviceable horse has become affected with whistling only in his gallop, and not in his trot, he does not suffer inconvenience from this pace, and he may advantageously, if suited to that kind of work, be put into harness; and although there may exist some little wheezing, a fair pace does not distress the animal; he may be usefully employed in harness-work, while his whistling will be drowned by the noise of the wheels: he is, however, UNSOUND.

WHEEZING.

See the article on "Whistling."

COUGH.

However simple or however recent in origin a cough may be, while it lasts the horse is UNSOUND.

It is of great importance that immediate attention be paid to the horse on the first symptoms of cough being noticed, while the cure is easy. The diseases to which horses are liable are, for the most part, rapid in progress; every hour of delay increases the difficulty, and in a short time the disease becomes developed in an acute or chronic form, condemning the horse to a life of base drudgery, and making him miserable to the end of his days.

CHRONIC COUGH.

While some horses, when laboring under chronic cough, are almost useless, others are but little inconvenienced and are as useful as ever: they are all, however, UNSOUND.

See the article on "Cough."

COLDS.

A horse suffering from cold in the head, which often produces whistling, is, for the nonce, UNSOUND.

See articles on "Cough" and "Whistling."

ASTHMA.

Asthma may be recognized by the short, soft cough that it produces. In some cases the inconvenience caused by this complaint is but slight, the horse giving merely a scarcely perceptible cough on coming out of or going into the stable, and the more in the winter than in summer: the extent of such cough depends upon the atmosphere and cleanliness of his box. Very commonly, horses touched with asthma do not cough when working, nor seem distressed like broken-winded horses.

Such horses often last many years, fulfilling the functions of their particular class, without inconvenience; yet, as there is chronic disease present, besides an assumed predisposition to injury of the lungs, they are

UNSOUND.

CRIB-BITING.

Crib-biting is a habit that some horses have, of taking hold of the manger with the teeth, or of resting the jaws upon it, accompanied by a disagreeable noise caused by sucking in and ejecting wind. It is a trick which horses sometimes learn of one another, but it is generally caused by neglect in providing work for these naturally active animals; by omitting, when young, to keep them, when unexercised, on a mouthing bit; and by allowing them to stand idle in the stable with no food before them, especially when their heads are tied up, so that they cannot amuse themselves by picking about in their beds.

The stomach of the horse has a natural tendency to keep distended, and therefore, if it be not replenished with food, it will become filled with air, and, 'if distended by too profuse a supply of the latter, will cause uncomfortable sensations to him: in which case, as he is, by nature, incapable of eructating; reason or instinct, whichever expression you prefer, induces him to adopt this method as the most effectual means of relieving himself from this inconvenience.

In its earlier stages, a little well-timed attention will cure a horse of this practice; and if he be in good condition, and his coat smooth, soft, and pliable, he is, in spite of this habit, SOUND.

As crib-biting will, in all probability, if not quickly checked, lead to serious results, specified in the following article, it may be deemed to be a VICE.

In the more advanced stages of crib-biting, neglect will have allowed the stomach and digestive organs to become affected, and the horse, being therefore diseased, will be UNSOUND.

In this latter stage of the disease the horse is thin, his coat stares or looks unthrifty, and his hide becomes tight; his cure is then difficult to effect, and is generally troublesome, if not impossible, to bring about.

PREVENTION OF CRIB-BITING (IN THE EARLY STAGES.)

Moderating the work will frequently cure horses of crib-biting, and will, where they appear weakly and out of order, and their coats "stare," (even though they be not crib-biters,) reinstate them in health. In the latter cases an earlier release for the night from work should be granted when circumstances allow.

EATING BEDS.

Many persons feel alarmed at their horses eating their beds; and very frequently in such cases grooms physic their horses with a view towards preventing this habit;

certainly, while the nausea resulting from the medicine lasts, the desired effect is produced; but, when the nausea is gone, the horse returns more ravenously than ever to the practice, and so, eventually, by repeated physickings, the healthy tone of the stomach is destroyed, and the refusal to eat sufficiently is met with extra medicine, in a vain attempt to restore the appetite which has been wantonly and foolishly damaged.

To such alarmists a few observations concerning this craving of the horse may be useful. I myself have been asked to provide some preventive for this habit, and my invariable answer has been,—" Keep better food before the horse; never let him stand too long without exercise or sufficient to eat, and you may depend upon finding that he will never eat his dirty bed."

If you follow this advice, you may be sure that he will not eat dirty straw, and that, if he does eat a little clean straw from his new bed, he does so only either when he finds an unthreshed ear, or when, having been too highly fed, he picks up a little to distend his stomach with something rather less nutritious than his accustomed fare.

Bed-eating is not a disease, and a horse with this habit can be warranted as SOUND.

And, as it is not attended by any real inconvenience, but is often a proof of good constitution, it is not even regarded as a VICE.

Arabs are delighted when they see a horse eat his own dung, saying that that is a proof that he will not starve.

More harm is done by letting horses stand too long without food than by putting too much before them; and although it is true that a ravenous horse does occasionally burst his stomach by excess in eating, as for instance, when he gets loose and finds out the corn-bin, yet such cases occur only when he has been much restricted in his diet, or has been worked for many hours, at a spell, without food. These cases are of very rare occurrence, and would be still more uncommon were proper and sufficient food regularly supplied.

Who has ever heard of a stage-coach horse, unstinted in his food, eating to this excess; or a horse at grass bursting himself in this manner?

Craving horses are the horses that should be selected for real work, but they are liable to become crib-biters if too stringent a rule be observed in the matter of food or exercise.

On the other hand, it is the horse having a delicate stomach, and not the hard-worker, that requires pampering and nursing, care being taken that he be not fed *ad nauseam.* Such a horse, on account of his indisposition to feed or work, does not show much evidence of past labor.

Except where under medical treatment, he is SOUND.

THE SOUND HORSE.

The sound horse is often too delicate to undergo an amount of work which distresses the legs, but he is nevertheless much coveted; while the useful horse, possessing good stamina, the power to work without causing pain to himself, and every evidence that he will long retain that power, is too often rejected, because he shows a few signs of past work.

Horse-buyers are too apt to be frightened at trifles through their ignorance of real and imaginary defects. When horses are being tried, it is no uncommon occurrence to see an animal brought out with a little enlargement upon some part of him. He is instantly rejected, with,—"I can never think of having that!" Another is brought forward that has some other trifling ailment, and he is sent back with the remark, "Put him in; that's quite enough!" A useless one may, probably, be brought forward next. He is sound, because there is not even a bump, speck, spot, or blemish upon him! He is accepted with—"That will do." The secret why such an one is so purchasable has to be learned. It is, however, most frequently the case that the horse has no pluck, or is too weak to hurt his limbs. He can never do a day's work, and costs more for nursing, petting, and physicking, than it would take to keep two useful ones; yet the latter are always "ready." For this reason, we must have a distinct class of horses: the second-hand horses, or the "used ones," as they are generally called,—and these should be warranted as "used horses,"—that is, as showing some signs of having done work. They will, however, be treated upon, and more particularly described, in another part of this work.

WIND-SUCKING.

This habit is somewhat similar to crib-biting, except that the horse does not take hold of anything, and that the noise frequently differs slightly. It is a species of crib-biting, and is more difficult to cure, as the horse is out of condition when it is addicted to wind-sucking. The muzzle is of no use in this case, and to effect a cure the same discipline must be observed as that recommended for crib-biting. Sometimes crib-biting degenerates into wind-sucking, which latter disease is caused by rubbing over the manger filthy and greasy messes, in order to prevent the horse from biting the wood. The disease of wind-sucking renders the horse UNSOUND.

WEAVING.

Weaving is a habit of moving from side to side in the stall, something in the manner of a weaver's shuttle, but really more like the restless habits of confined animals in a menagerie. Weaving is generally contracted through idleness, and is frequently learnt on board ship. Weavers are mostly nervous horses, full of energy, good workers, and SOUND.

TO CURE WEAVING.

The same steps may be taken to cure weaving, as are mentioned in the preceding article: in addition, it is well to fasten the horse with two pillar reins attached respectively to each side of the halter, and tight enough to prevent him from swinging or swaying.

DULLNESS.

Having examined the more general reasons for rejecting horses at sale, we have now to consider causes of secondary importance, yet such as must receive attention.

The nostril is one of the most important parts of the horse to be attended to: it is much overlooked. There are many horses that are called dull, sorry jades, who will be found to go for a short distance good-humoredly and at a good pace, and then draw in, bearing a severe punishment rather than improve their pace. "What a dull, lazy brute it is!" cries its owner, but in reality he is neither dull nor lazy. The cause of his difficulty lies in the smallness of his nostril, which is not sufficiently large to permit enough air to pass up for purifying the blood as it passes through the animal's lungs. The consequence is, that with every increase of speed the animal suffers acute pain. This too small nostril is the cause of slowness or dullness in all inferiorly-bred horses.

Where horses are well-bred, dullness is more likely to arise from a contraction of the bones than from a diminutive nostril.

Where speed and continuous labor, therefore, are required, the above two provocations to dullness should be well looked into: even in thorough-bred horses we find some imperfection or other; and it should be borne in mind that a horse falling short of qualities sufficient for making him a first-rate racer, may make a good country hunter, or hackney. For the hundredth time I say— Adapt a horse to the work best suited to his condition, and all will be well. Of course this plan will sometimes alter a horse's class, but, being equal to the work of the class into which he is drafted, he is   SOUND.

Where disease creates dullness, he is   UNSOUND.

MALFORMATIONS.

Malformations are not an unsoundness unless the horse is diseased or lame, or is prevented from doing the work of the class to which he belongs.

Where there is any doubt of the horse's ability to stand the work of his class upon the supposition that the affected part has not been permanently healed, the buyer is naturally anxious to try the horse before he purchases it. Now, as there seems to be very absurd ideas entertained by many persons as to what may be done with horses on trial, and as the subject is of much importance to both buyer and seller, perhaps I cannot do better than devote some space to it.

THE TRIAL.

Having satisfied yourself upon the general merits of the horse, try him, and, whilst trying him, use him fairly, according to the treatment to which horses of his class and condition are subjected. Thus, suppose you are in want of a horse able to trot twelve miles an hour, and upon trial of one you put him to that pace without the consent of the owner, in such case, should any accident or subsequent illness occur or be presumed to occur to the horse as the result of the trial, you may be made to take him at the price agreed upon before starting (and a price should be always agreed upon), or you may be made to pay the damage done to him, should the owner feel disposed to compel you so to do. It may seem inconsistent that you should not be permitted to risk accidents, with penalty for their occurrence, by trying a horse at the full speed he should go as one of his class; but as there may be so many interpretations put upon what is a just and what an unjust trial, it is best to have with you at the time the owner or his agent; for if you took the horse further than you were authorized to do by the owner, if you drove it faster, or took it over a different road than the one stipulated, and did this in the absence of the owner or his representative, you would have to pay the cost of any damage done to the animal; but not so if the owner were with you, and he made no objection to your methods of operation.

Again, if you state that you want a saddle-horse, and receive such an one, but instead of using him for the saddle, you try him in harness; for any accidents accruing therefrom you will be liable; so that if you only mark him with the collar, or in any other trifling way, nay, should you rub off a few hairs so as to interfere with the immediate sale of the horse, or depreciate his price, the owner can insist upon your taking him off his hands or paying for the injury done.

If you want a saddle horse, and try him as you would a hunter, then are you liable for accidents, although they may occur at another part of the trial, because it may be that the improper exertion to which he has been subjected may have conduced to the accident.

A particular condition, to be acquired only by a certain treatment or training, will enable the horse to accomplish any extraordinary work, as in the case of the racer, the hunter, and the trotter. But the further removed he is from his legitimate work, so much greater is the chance of the animal's being ruined, even when exercised for a short time only. You should also bear in mind that horses for sale are generally in the very worst possible condition to bear fatigue: they are got up to catch the eye and are made as soft and sleek as possible. In the "selling state" they are, so to speak, all fat; in their "trained state," all muscle. It is the opinion of many horse-buyers that horses should always be in a "trained condition;" but the simple and ordinary requirements of commercial transactions render this, generally, impossible. The trotter is the horse kept nearest this state of training, being mostly in the hands of those who possess only one horse, and who are consequently always putting their animal to the trial. A really sound trotter is, therefore, a most uncommon thing: the exceptions must be sought in those studs where trotters are kept only as match horses and for short distances. Trotters are of all horses the most tried—the most overtried. Many indifferent horsemen would have no hesitation at driving the trotter, but they would as soon attempt to fly as to mount the racer.

Neither extreme is good. Horses should not be too much worn when sold, and they certainly should not be got up to such a pitch of sleekness and delicacy that attacks of inflammation or other diseases would be attended by more than ordinary danger to the animal. Dealers of course would prefer keeping their horses in a more rugged and vigorous condition, but hitherto buyers have looked at horses as butchers do at oxen, and valued them in proportion to the amount of fat they carry. Of course this is an error; but improvement is beginning, for the dealers in live meat do certainly look for many things now besides fat, and they are right.

Perhaps this place is as good as any other to remark upon the absurdity of buying an animal that had once in his life performed a particular feat, instead of seeking to possess horses of capacity for general usefulness. As well accept for man-servant a decrepid old man who once in his life was most active and had done the state some service. Choose a horse, as you would a man, for his ability and willingness; then husband his resources, and you may have a good and faithful servant for many years.

SURFEIT.

Should surfeit amount to more than a few spots upon the outside of the quarters, particularly the hind quarters, it is of little consequence. If you are desirous of having the horse, but from the number of spots upon him you apprehend farcy, it will be advisable in making the bargain to stipulate for a cure of the disease within a fortnight. With proper treatment, the mere surfeit may be cured in that time. Until cured, however, the horse is UNSOUND.

BLEEDING.

Accepting the definition of soundness that it is perfect health, whilst every deviation is indicative of unsoundness, then the simple necessity for drawing blood renders the horse unsound, and consequently, until the orifice made by the lancet is healed, he is UNSOUND.

MEDICINE.

To require a dose of medicine is an UNSOUNDNESS; therefore, as in the case last mentioned, until the effects of the medicine are removed, the horse is UNSOUND.

DIET AND EXERCISE.

Requiring a particular treatment of either diet or exercise—a treatment widely different from that which is ordinarily adopted—is a deviation from soundness.

DEALERS' HORSES.

After studying the preceding part of this book, more particularly the contents of the three last paragraphs, the question may naturally arise—"How is it possible that dealers' horses pass at all; for, certainly in the case of high-priced horses, attention must be paid to every little nicety with a view towards securing sound animals?" It is just this, that as the buyer compels the vendor to keep his horses in a state so highly "finished," the buyer must make allowances or he will never effect a purchase.

If a horse is capable of undergoing the trial as well as other horses in the same adipose state, being, in all other respects, just as he should be according to the rules laid down in this work, then he is SOUND.

Nobody but the purchaser is to blame for a horse, with no one perceptible defect, having around it as it were an atmosphere of doubt and uncertainty; but where he does not mean to put the horse immediately to work, but intends to bring him to it properly by degrees, the animal will not suffer. But if horses newly purchased from the dealer's hands are at once put to work without due consideration, some severe disease often accrues, which, if it does not kill them off, may render them cripples for life. When this really occurs—and it is by no means unfrequent, the purchaser blames the vendor, who does not deserve it, because, were he not to keep his horses in the finest possible condition, he could not command a high price for them. This accounts for the general complaint of the difficulty in obtaining good saddle horses.

SADDLE HORSES.

To make a good saddle horse is a work of time, and during the process of training he must be ridden by good horsemen who know what they are about. To break him in well, you will subject him to many little accidents; and certain little things, the result of the exercise, will be sure to make their appearance, which will be construed to be the result of work. Over-fastidious buyers will often be thus deceived, and reject a well-trained saddle horse for a sleeker animal whose action is not set. Therefore let it be noted as a fact that until certain crotchets and fancied imperfections are overlooked, and are no longer bugbears, we shall want good saddle horses. Those who are fortunate enough to possess such a treasure will not part with it until it is fairly worn out; nor would a dealer be at the trouble of producing another, unless he could insure for it a price commensurate with the pains required for the operation.

It is a common complaint that the horses of the present day do not lift their feet sufficiently high, in the same way that they did when saddle horses were more perfect, this fault in them being erroneously attributed to their breed. The thorough-bred horse may oe taught to lift his leg as high and bend his knee as well as any other, even after he has been trained for racing; and he then is better than the old-fashioned saddle horse, because safer and easier, and his breed renders him capable of doing more work.

HUNTERS.

After reading the above remarks upon saddle horses, you may naturally ask, How is it, then, that we have good hunters now in some portions of the country? It is because known hunters are seldom offered for sale in a pursy state; or, if they are in such a condition at any time, they undergo a thorough training before they are set to work. The remark also applies to young horses that are bought for the purpose of making hunters: it would indeed be a raw hand that would take a fat hunter into the field.

Again, hunters are known, and exchange hands upon their merits. Who ever refused the best horse in the hunt because he had windgalls, enlarged hocks, or any of the thousand and one objections made to other and unknown horses? If the hunter is capable of performing cleverly the various standard feats of the hunting-field, many an imperfect piece of his symmetry is overlooked.

"Besides," remarks some one, "broken knees in the hunter are not of any consequence." From this I beg to dissent. Of all the horses I should least like the hunter to be a tumble-down, and for this good reason:—the shoulders of the tumble-down are upright, so that at particular leaps he can not extend his fore-legs sufficiently to come down on his fore-feet, and most likely when he thus over-jumps himself, he comes down head first. I am confident there never was an instance of the rider being killed by his horse rolling heels over head upon him unless that horse were upright in his shoulders. Although I hate any horse approaching to a tumble-down for any purpose whatever, I should prefer that a saddle horse should fall with me on the road, though he should cut himself to pieces, rather than I would risk leaping with an upright-shouldered hunter. In severe leaps there is more force required than in ordinary riding, and therefore the obliquity is more needed. But I would rather avoid both. I hate the action of these horses.

VICES.

In speaking of the vices of horses, we must first observe that a warranty of soundness does not infer that the horse is free from vice, unless such be particularly expressed. Next, you must bear in mind that a very vicious horse may be a very sound one, and that, too, because perhaps on account of his bad habits his owners may have been afraid of using him.

Vice may be either that which is dangerous to those who have to do with the animal, being confined to either the stable, to the work generally, or to only one particular kind of work; or it may be of a nature to effect only the horse himself, or his master in a pecuniary point of view, by lessening the value. Of such last may be mentioned wind-suckers, crib-biters, weavers, horses having a determined trick of getting loose in the stable, (although there may be a certain degree of innocence in their mischief,) for they may be the cause of injury to themselves or others.

Kicking one another, or at people, either in their work or at any other time, if with ill nature, is a   VICE.

Biting one another, or those about them, unless in

play, or whatever trick tends to the injury of themselves or others, is a VICE.

In the first or most serious class of vices may be enumerated—kicking and biting in or out of the stable; kicking at the leg of the rider or driver, either when mounting into the saddle or at any other time; or rearing, or running away, or rubbing the rider's leg against anything, or lying down when wanted to proceed, or falling on the side, or stopping suddenly when in a fast pace, or violently insisting upon going to any place that the horse happens to have been at before. Jibbing, or refusing to proceed, is a vice: so is backing against the owner's will, or turning round with violence when not required so to do, unless this results from mismanagement of the user. A refusal to stand still in order to be mounted, if from ill nature, may be classed under this head. Bucking or raising the back when mounted, and then putting the head between the fore-legs and jumping, is a disagreeable and dangerous vice; so is the trick of swelling out the body till either the girths or straps to which they are buckled give way. If horses are guilty of any of the vices here enumerated and have been sold as well-broken horses, warranted free from vice, they are returnable. The half-broken colt may be guilty of some of these habits without being vicious; but thenceforth it depends upon the way of procedure.

This being merely a catalogue of vices, some of them will be more particularly described under their respective headings, together with their causes, effects, and remedies, in order that buyers may know where certain vices are barred, or whether they amount to a reason for the total rejection of the horse or not.

Should you, however, put a horse into harness without having a guarantee that he is quiet to drive, and he then proves guilty of one or more of the active vices, you cannot return him.

'Warranted quiet in harness" bars all injurious vices affecting that particular work. There is one vice, however, said to be questionable, although I doubt it; that is "jibbing," or refusing to move when required to do so. But where the horse runs back, there can be no doubt about the vice proving dangerous and a bar to a perfect warranty. Lying down, another trick of a jibber, is also a dangerous vice, if only on account of the shafts, independently of other and personal risks. Also, where the horse, after standing awhile, goes off with a violent rush, rear, or plunge, there can be no doubt of the danger (except in skillful hands), or of the vice. This also requires some qualification, as a mere jump, lift, or start at a canter may be magnified by the timid. Again, it is a query whether it is not the coachman, rather than the horse, that is in fault; and in the former case the horse is not do be held to be vicious.

A horse may be quiet in harness, yet very vicious and dangerous out of it, either in the stable or to ride. These are not included in a warranty of "quiet in harness," because in the last two cases he is out of the harness. "Free from vice," added to "quiet in harness," signifies that the animal is also quiet in the stable. He may, however, be vicious to ride, so that where he is wanted for this purpose also, "to ride" must be added in the warranty, as the seller may contend that he sold him for harness only.

The receipts hereafter given will show how all these difficulties may be overcome.

A simple warranty of soundness does not necessarily imply quietness. A horse may be as vicious as possible, so much so as to become almost useless, and at the same time not render himself returnable. "Free from vice or any general inclination to do mischief," alludes to the stable as well as to the work of the horse. Still he may not be well broken, as this does not imply that he is so or otherwise; therefore, the being thus untutored would not make him returnable. But, if, though unbroken, he has acquired bad tricks or vices, he is returnable. Add "quiet to ride," and he must perform this. He may, nevertheless, not be broken further than just to "back," as it is termed—that is, to allow any one to be upon his back with the saddle while he carries him about. The phrase, a "good back," "good hunter," "ladies' horse," "ménage," or "quiet in harness," or for whatever other purpose he may be required, should be specified. As an assistance, I give a few forms of receipt, which may be easily adapted to suit any purpose required.

RECEIPTS ON WARRANTIES.

May, 18—.

Received of   , for a gelding, warranted sound, free from vice, and quiet to ride or drive, five hundred dollars.—A. B.

N. B.—This includes the commonest purpose, with quietness both within and without doors; also soundness. Any qualification may be left out or added; as for example:—

June, 18—.

Received of   , two hundred dollars, for a chestnut mare, warranted sound, with the exception of a slightly enlarged hock—quiet to ride.—B. C.

The hock being the only exception, should there be any other unsoundness, the purchaser can return the horse; but not for vice, as that is not mentioned; neither is harness-work. Both of these, therefore, are at the buyer's risk.

July, 18—.

Received of   , three hundred dollars, for a brown horse, warranted sound, with the exception of an enlargement at the back of the near hock, on which he goes at present free from lameness. A good hunter. C. D.

Any other unsoundness vitiates this warranty; or if it can be proved that he went lame on the excepted hock at the time of trial, he is returnable. Here he is only for one purpose, and may not be worth anything for any other work. But if he fulfills the warranty by being a good hunter, he does all that can be naturally expected of him. Good hunters are often useless for hackney-work.

August, 18—.

Received of   , two hundred dollars, for a gray gelding, warranted sound, with the exception of   , and upon which I warrant he has gone sound from   to and up to the time of my giving this receipt. He is quiet in harness and a good hackney. D. E.

Here the warranty, as far as the doubtful part, runs back to given time—upon the length of time that the horse has gone free from inconvenience, and you place your reliance upon his continuing to do so. If, therefore, you find that he has been lame on the excepted part within the period named, he is returnable, but not otherwise —this defect of lameness having been particularly specified in the warranty.

It will be readily perceived that any particular vice, vices, or defects, whether of eyes, limbs, wind, etc., etc., may be thus excepted; therefore, one more example will suffice.

September, 18—.

Received of   , the sum of   dollars, for a black horse, sixteen hands high, warranted sound, with the exception of an enlargement on the off forefoot, but upon which he has gone sound during the whole of the last three months, since its formation. He is six years old.

HEIGHT AND AGE.

The last form is also a warranty of age—that he is past his fifth and not yet in his seventh year; for horses never alter less than one year at a time. If you can prove he has not arrived at his sixth year, or that he has entered his seventh, you can, if you are so disposed, return the horse.

You will perceive that this last receipt is for a horse—meaning thereby an entire one—neither gelding nor mare. His height is also mentioned; but if you have any particular reason for stating his exact height, it must be on the special warranty placed after the word "height," and not before it, or it will be presumed that you might have had him measured at the time of purchase. In order to avoid quibbling, it is the best way, where a given height is required, to put the horse under the standard. Even then there is much sleight of hand going on. Strict attention must, therefore, be paid if you are in any way particular to an inch. From the foregoing observations it will be seen that a simple warranty—"free from vice," applies to the stable only; to be quiet in his work, and each particular kind of work, must be specified, as in the first receipt.

QUIET IN HARNESS.

"Warranted quiet in harness" does not imply the long usage of a horse to that particular kind of work, or that he has become particularly handy. All that it engages is that the horse has been used sufficiently to prove that any coachman of tolerable ability may drive him without accident. Therefore, after buying a horse thus warranted, before you put yourself to any expense in returning him on account of an accident, be sure the accident was not caused through your own negligence. A little negligence or mismanagement may do a great deal of mischief. Too rough a hand upon a sensitive mouth, or a little nervousness or improper treatment in the driving, or inattention to the harness, may be all the fault, and, after being put to great expense and inconvenience, you may still be obliged to retain the horse, as all those things that seemed the effect of vice have been occasioned by want of skill.

A chance kick or rear, if merely in play, as is generally the case when the animal is too fresh or in the habit of looking or playing on seeing certain objects (which some would term shying), is not a vice, and does not render the horse returnable, where it can be proved that he was in a good humor or wanted work. Any mischief that might result would be at the risk of the buyer. But where the seller allows any one to try a horse in harness, whilst thus too fresh, without giving a caution, all mischief that ensues falls upon the vendor's shoulders. Where this caution is given, he must either be a very good or a very foolhardy coachman to be his own driver until the seller has driven a little of this play out of him.

SHYING.

When horses shy, it is either from unsoundness, play, or vice. It is generally occasioned by disease in the eye: cataract is the most common. Should the horse start at a little water or froth lying in the road, you may almost depend upon this disease being present, even though it exists in the shape of a speck no bigger than a pin's point. After cataracts are formed in the eye, that part of the pupil which is affected becomes opaque. Cataracts vary from the smallest specks to the obliteration or total opacity of the pupil, the shying increasing up to the last stage of blindness. Inflammation or cold in the eye will also produce shying. Every one of these stages, from the slightest inflammation to complete blindness of the affected eye or eyes, makes the horse

UNSOUND.

When there is no inflammation present, the various diseases of this organ are easily detected, as well as the injury which the eyes have received from the imflammations they have already undergone; but as this is only to be acquired by practice, it will be unnecessary for me to occupy further space in attempting to explain that which would not assist those who are not already acquainted with the eye under all circumstances. I would merely observe, as a general rule, that the eyes of those horses most subject to disorder appear small, and the upper lid wrinkled: they are termed "buck-eyed." Every stage of shying proceeding from disease is an

UNSOUNDNESS.

Not so where it is a matured habit produced by either a nervous or brutal user; in that case it is a   VICE.

It is not, however, a vice till it becomes a confirmed habit, because if, during the early stages the horse changes into judicious hands, he ceases to do wrong.

Patience, and care in riding and driving will soon cure this.

When the horse starts or plays from want of exercise, or from a sudden noise, of an unusual kind, or where it arises from standing in a dark stable, provided that the eyes are not seriously injured, and that the pupils soon contract from the dilatation the dark has occasioned to their natural size, he is free from vice and   SOUND.

To keep him sound the purchaser must put him into a lighter stable, when his eyes will keep right, and he will not shy; but if he be kept in the dark, disease will soon follow, and the animal will be, consequently, rendered

UNSOUND.

In the two last cases the horse is free from vice.

Young horses occasionally shy from having chronic dilatation of the pupils, and are then **UNSOUND**.

But where such dilatation is not chronic, as shown above, the defect is soon removed.

Where the dilatation is the natural effect of age alone, if the horse merely looks or glances at objects without jumping or turning so as to occasion inconvenience, he is **SOUND**.

But if he stops suddenly, jumps to one side, or turns round quickly, whether resulting from defective sight, disease, old age, or any combination of these causes, the horse is **UNSOUND**.

STARTING.

Starting is a **VICE**.
See articles on "Shying" and "Bolting."

BOLTING—RUNNING AWAY.

Bolting, or running away, is a serious **VICE**.
This does not, however, apply to the young horse when he jumps suddenly at any object that appears in a quiet by-road, or when he looks curiously at anything strange to him; he may even, under such circumstances, move over askew to the other side of the road, but this must not be considered to be a vice. Good riding is all that such a horse requires.

If his eyes are perfect, he is **SOUND**.

PLAY—PLAYFULNESS.

Gamboling and good-humored play, resulting from plenty of ease, are not detrimental to the horse's value, and they are easily got rid of, or, at the least, lessened by a little exercise.

They may be considered to be, generally, a proof of a strong and vigorous state of health.

A true horseman does not think any the worse of a horse for his playfulness; but as a nervous person might be alarmed at this habit, and put himself to some expense in trying to effect a return of the horse to the vendor, it is well to add that, as playfulness is not a vice, the horse is not, on that account, returnable.

But such a temper in a horse as is decidedly capricious or mischievous constitutes a VICE.

The act of a horse looking slily or askance at any objects that happen to catch his eye, while he is passing, must not be mistaken for shying; for the indecision of the rider's hand will convey a feeling of fear to the horse's mind through the effect of the bridle upon the mouth, while the horse will frequently anticipate the approach of a danger which is, in fact, imaginary, by feeling an undue pressure, or a sudden and undecided loosening or tremulous motion of the rider's legs or knees. He is, consequently, suddenly alarmed, fancies that the very first object which he meets is the cause of the supposed danger, and tries, as instinct prompts him, to avoid it.

If a horse that has been ridden by a nervous rider for a few times only be taken in hand by a thorough and clever-handed horseman, it will be found that he will recover his self-confidence in a very few days' work. It is a fault of greater or less magnitude, according to the time that may be required for its eradication, and therefore, until the cure be effected, and it be certain that no injury will accrue from past mismanagement, such a fault is a VICE.

The horse that will not even step over a straw, when ridden by an undecided and hesitating rider, will frequently take any leap with him who rides with a cool determination and a steady hand: so that, when the horse has contracted no permanent habit, but shies only while he is ridden in a nervous manner, as the fault is not in the horse, but in the master, the act of so shying does not constitute a VICE.

Vice does not always render the animal returnable to the vendor. If, through nervousness or any fault in management, you induce the horse to shy, you must not, on that account, attribute any blame to him; and, in order to enable you to succeed in effecting a return of the animal, you must be in a position to prove that he was, under proper management, addicted to shying previous to your purchasing him. *Facilis decensus averni!* Bad habits are far easier to inculcate or to acquire than good ones.

It is easy to sell or to buy a horse, be he good or bad, but impossible to furnish, or acquire suddenly, the art of managing him properly.

The above remarks as to the ease with which a horse contracts a habit of shying apply with equal force to all other habits which may be induced in him, either inside or outside the stable; such as biting, kicking, plunging, jibbing, savaging, etc.

SKITTISHNESS.

Horses that are highly fed, and at the same time underworked, frequently acquire a way of spasmodic starting and playfulness, and are then called skittish; such horses being, by the uninitiated, not uncommonly called shiers. As the skittishness goes off on the horse being put to serious and hard work, it is not to be deemed a VICE.

MEDICINE.

A dose of medicine given to a horse, even though he require it, may make him unsound, until the physic has ceased to affect him. Under the same category of specifics, I must include training, and sweating to get down some of the superfluous fat; all trainers, however, know that these processes may be overdone. Any deviation from health is an UNSOUNDNESS.

Until the effect of the medicine has passed off, there is such a deviation from health, as is proved by the altered pulse, the derangement of appetite, and general dullness. Besides, owing to the great susceptibility of the stomach of the horse, until the effect has ceased, the ultimate result is uncertain; a dose, innocuous to one horse, being often almost, if not quite, fatal to another.

It is better understood now than it was formerly, that, if the medicine, in proper quantities and at right times, has been administered to the horse, either to qualify him for work different from that to which he has been accustomed, or to restore him to his usual condition; as, for instance, on his return from grass, or on the commencement of his preparation for racing or hunting, and, if you can be satisfied that the dose was moderate, not injurious in its properties, and administered to the horse at the time when he was in a proper state of perparation to receive it, there is no great risk in purchasing him. I should not have gone so lengthily into the subject of caution requisite in these cases, were it not that many still adhere to the system of giving a ball consisting of calomel (a medicine rarely necessary), and other drugs sufficient to ruin all the horses in a whole troop of cavalry.

We cannot wonder, when we recollect the preposterous doses that were habitually given to horses a few years ago, that they often either destroyed the poor creatures, or rendered them permanently decrepit.

It does not occur every day that there is any necessity to buy a horse when still under the effects of physic; yet there are cases when, from rivalry among those who know him, anxiety is manifested to purchase a horse who would not, under other circumstances, be or be likely to be sold; and in such instances the successful competitor runs considerable risk.

In spite of the unimportance in many cases, I think it right to show what dangers and chances may occasionally happen, as I have often been questioned on the subject.

A short time since, two gentlemen were, at the same time, considering about buying a horse that was just then in physic, with a view to the preparation for a match in which he was engaged. One of the gentlemen had offered to purchase the horse as soon as the medicine had worked off: the other, in the meantime, consulted me as to what consequences might be apprehended, and, after I had examined the horse, and had satisfied myself as to his appearance, bought the horse, much to the chagrin of his more cautious rival.

STRANGLES.

It is frequently a matter for deliberation whether it would be advisable to buy a horse laboring under strangles (in whatever stage the disease may happen to be), or, in some cases, whether it would be prudent to purchase a horse which, though not actually afflicted with this disease at the time, yet shows symptoms of its approach.

In aged horses the appearance of strangles must be noted with some suspicion, as the horse generally has the disease while young, and very rarely more than once, while the older horse is more subject to glanders, which is sometimes mistaken for strangles. Strangles may so debilitate an old horse as to degenerate into glanders.

Strangles is a disease which, if properly attended to on its first appearance, rarely terminates fatally in the result denoted by the name: such a result is a very scarce exception to the general rule—recovery.

While the horse is under the influence of strangles, he is   UNSOUND.

In order to prevent mistakes, it would be an improvement, where there is the least suspicion of strangles, to have the warranty qualified by the addition of the words, "Except the strangles."

This disease is curable within a few days; it rarely attacks old horses.

COLDS.

Cold in the head, of long standing, may be mistaken by those not conversant with the disease, for strangles, while it is, in fact, the worse of the two, and is of a far more serious nature than most people imagine. While the comparatively innocuous disease, strangles, is much dreaded, cold, until it shows its seriousness by extreme running, is thought lightly of.

Cold, if long neglected, frequently degenerates into glanders; in any case, while the horse is suffering from it, he is   UNSOUND.

GLANDERS.

Glanders, which bears a very similar appearance to that of strangles, is a complaint of the very worst character.

Glanders runs for years, if it does not, in the interim, terminate in death.

It is easily communicated either by inoculation or imbibition; its contagiousness, however, is very doubtful, as sound horses have been known to stand for years in the same stables with glandered ones without contracting the disease; indeed, sound and glandered horses have been known to work together without the disease being communicated.

Common causes of the disease are—overwork, an insufficient quantity of nutritious food, debility, and foul, close stables.

Where the precaution laid down at the end of the article on "Strangles" has been observed, and there is no longer a doubt that the disease is of a more serious nature than that of strangles, the horse should be returned to the vendor, the chance of effecting a cure being very small; besides, there is danger of the attendant becoming inoculated, the expense of promoting the cure is heavy, and the time that will elapse before the horse is sound and fit for work is considerable.

Glanders is seldom accompanied by any cough, but one nostril is generally, in the early stages, affected, there being a running from the nose of a glandered horse of a more glue-like or colloid nature than that in strangles; and it is useful to know that while the matter that runs from the nose in the former disease sinks in water, that which flows in strangles and cold, floats.

Until the disease has made some progress, the horse appears to be in good health, and his eyes bright and clear; but it is prudent not to place too much reliance upon this absence of symptoms. The moment that you have any grounds for suspicion, procure a donkey or some other animal of little value—even a rabbit—and let him be inoculated with the matter; a few hours will decide whether the disease is or is not present. Should glanders be unmistakably discovered, the sooner both animals are destroyed the better.

The inoculation of the donkey with the suspicious matter is not an inhuman act; for it is only the possible sacrifice of one life, to insure the preservation of we know not how many. Even the lives of the attendants are at stake, as it is well known that the reception of glandered matter in the slightest scratch or abrasion of the skin is almost certain to terminate fatally.

Although the difference between cold, strangles, and glanders is sufficiently marked to be generally distinguished, yet no description of them will render it safe for the uninitiated to decide with certainty which disease it is.

The best plan is to put alone by themselves all horses afflicted with strangles or severe cold in the head, particularly if they have been recently purchased; this will, at all events, prevent any chance of glanders, if present, being communicated to the other horses.

It is hardly necessary to add that a glandered horse is
UNSOUND.

BASTARD-STRANGLES, OR VIVES.

When a horse has not had the strangles at the usual time, that is, generally, between the second and fourth year, he is frequently attacked by this disease, being in fact the strangles delayed till a later period of life than usual: Vives really meaning a revival of the attack, which is frequently called by old farriers, bastard-strangles, or vives, and which is a more obstinate complaint than true strangles.

Vives is not often, in itself, fatal, nor difficult to cure, if attended to without delay; but, if neglected, it is often followed by very serious results, such as broken-wind, or even glanders; it is originated by a severe cold too long neglected.

The accompanying cough is more violent than that in strangles.

A horse laboring under vives or bastard-strangles is
UNSOUND.

Should you have bought the horse with an expressed

understanding that the disease under which he is laboring was the strangles only, and that he was, in other respects, sound, you may return him if the complaint is found to be the vives, on the score of his not fulfilling the conditions of the warranty.

BENT BEFORE.

When the fore-legs of the horse are bent forward at the knee, he is said to be bent before: this may proceed from overwork, or from pain in the feet resulting from contraction, inflammation, etc., but it more frequently proceeds from flat feet. In these cases, the animal is UNSOUND.

When the cause does not consist in pain, and when the deviation from the natural line is but slight, and the horse can do his proper work without inconvenience, even then, as in the case of total blindness, the defect may be visible, but he is SOUND.

When the profile of the fore-legs has a deviation of anything more than the very slightest, it is a BLEMISH.

You must not be talked over into the belief that the horse was deformed to this extent when he was foaled, and that it is not, therefore, the result of hard work or mismanagement, for though all colts are foaled crooked, or bent before, they remain so for a short time only.

Bent-legged horses have a reputation for good courage; if they are bent but slightly, they are frequently safe and good saddle-horses. They are, however, best adapted to harness-work; and, when much bent, should be worked in double harness, so that they may be free from any weight on the back.

UPRIGHT SHOULDERS.

Horses may be sound and yet unsafe to ride.

Amongst these are such as have upright shoulders, which result in some instances from bent legs.

Horses of this kind are in this respect perfectly sound, as much as the blind horse is; for in the former, as well as the latter case, the defect is plainly visible. Though a very upright-shouldered horse is considered unsound in so far as regards his capabilities as a hunter, he is, nevertheless, able to do harness-work, without inconvenience or danger, and, as long as he is kept for that kind of work only, is SOUND.

Many writers contend that upright shoulders are necessary to even first-class draught. I differ from them. But the horse being misplaced does not render him unsound.

In thus alluding to his unfitness for hunting purposes, I take an extreme of upright shoulders: though there is danger in every degree of this make, that is, in every gradation, from the oblique or perfect contour, down to extreme and most faulty deformity.

Therefore, horses with upright shoulders are, properly speaking, suitable for harness-work only; the nearer the shoulders approach to uprightness, the greater is the decrease in the horse's speed, until at length he is qualified for slow work only; so long as he has speed enough left in him for his required labor, he is well adapted for double harness or for four-wheel work, as there is then no vertical pressure of his back.

When such horses fall down, which they are almost certain to do before the ninth year, if working fast, and they hurt themselves in a trifling degree only, they are, until cured, UNSOUND.

Soundness and unsoundness, subsequent to such a fall, depends entirely upon the extent of the injury received. See the article on "Broken Knees."

UPRIGHT JOINTS—KNUCKLING.

When the pastern-joint of one or both of the fore-legs is perpendicular to the rest of the leg, instead of sloping

backwark, if this defect arise from work, the animal is
UNSOUND.

Such a deformity, in itself a serious defect, is bad also on account of its being such a deviation from nature as will soon render the horse useless from the lameness resulting from the concussion that the altered structure of the joints permits. Sometimes this knuckling is produced by overwork or strains; sometimes by pumice soles; and very often it arises from navicular disease.

Where either of the latter two exists, the disease is, of itself, an UNSOUNDNESS.

With the hind-legs, these observations do not hold good; for a horse may be quite upright in the joints of the hind-legs, and yet be perfectly SOUND.

A horse in this case is almost invariably as well able as any other to do his work: for it must be observed that nature often makes these joints much more upright than those of the fore-legs, because in the latter a greater degree of elasticity is required to break concussion, as there is greater weight borne by them than by the hind ones. The rest of the fore-leg is, of necessity, of a pillar-like form, to enable it to support the weight of the fore-quarters in action, as well as the additional weight and concussion produced by the propeller-like motion of the hind-legs, and, therefore, the foreleg is possessed of few or no spring appliances beyond what are contained in the pastern and foot.

The loss of even the slightest spring which is conducive to the prevention of concussion is, evidently, a serious matter; how much more serious must be the deprivation of this, the largest and most important spring of all.

As the hind-legs have not the weight of the head and neck to support, they are not required to be upright or column-like. For their function is the propelling of the body; and, with a view to effecting this with speed, they are of necessity longer than the fore ones.

I think it is needless for me to enter into reasons further than to say that, for the convenience of the animal, and with a view to his adaptability to his work, his hind-legs are bent, and therefore full of springs, which render the hind-feet much less liable to the many diseases to which the fore ones are prone; indeed, so rarely are the hind-feet affected by navicular disease, pumice sole, or the various evils resulting from concussion, that, when such maladies do appear, they may be considered as extraordinary exceptions to the rule.

We may then be justified in saying that horses do not have these diseases in their hind-feet, and that, consequently, there is less use made of the pastern joints here, than in the fore-feet.

If the knuckling does not interfere with the action of the horse (however unsightly the defect may be), he is
SOUND.

But such unsightliness is considered to be a
BLEMISH.

When the uprightness impedes the action of the horse, or renders him incapable of performing the work due from one of his class, he is
UNSOUND.

KNUCKLING.

Though uprightness and knuckling are frequently used indiscriminately for the same fault, some persons make the distinction, that the former consists in perpendicularity, while the latter implies "bending over" at the pastern-joint. If there is any difference between the two, knuckling may be considered to be the more aggravated form. A horse that knuckles over is
UNSOUND.

ENLARGED JOINTS.

Enlarged joints, resulting from blows, sprains, and wounds on the pastern-joints of the hind-legs, are generally contracted in the field, and are, therefore, most common in hunters, and mostly on the hind-legs, the proximate cause being that the rider, by holding on by the bridle during the leap, prevents him thereby from throwing up his legs sufficiently to clear the fence.

Those horses which have much timber or wall-jumping to do are the most subject to these defects.

If there is no raw place, but a scar only; if the skin has completely grown over the injured part; and if the enlargement has arrived at its full size, and become hard and bony, so as not to interfere with the horse's action and capacity to perform his usual work, he may he held to be SOUND.

The enlargement is a BLEMISH.

See the article on "Spavins," "Curbs," etc.

SOFT ENLARGEMENTS.

During the formation of soft enlargements, and until their result is ascertained, the horse is UNSOUND.

If, upon their being fully developed, they do not impede the horse in the execution of his work, he is SOUND.

But, when they are so large as to be unsightly, they are BLEMISHES.

See articles on "Windgalls," "Thorough-pins," "Bog-spavin," "Curbs," and "Spavins."

LONG PASTERNS.

When long pasterns do not impair the horse's action, by causing weakness, as described in the articles "Cutting" and "Speedy-cut," he is SOUND.

Long pasterns, except when they are extreme for the weight or work required, may be considered an advantage, as they are easy to the rider and prevent concussion to the horse.

If the length of the pasterns arises from the rupture or unnatural elongation of the tendon, the horse is then termed "broken down," and is UNSOUND.

When, from the great length of the pastern, the horse is incapable of doing the work due from one of his class, even though he was so foaled, he must be considered
UNSOUND.

Very long-pasterned horses, when they turn out their toes considerably, are sometimes called "Dancing-masters."

BOOTS.

Many a horse is unable to do his proper work without striking one leg against another; this fault arises either from weakness and malformation, or from the horse having, during breaking, been allowed to acquire a crooked, slovenly gait.

Such a horse, on account of his requiring the constant use of boots to prevent injury and cutting by striking his legs together, and on account of his demanding extra care, is UNSOUND.

If from temporary weakness, or from leg-weariness caused by over-work or poverty of condition, the horse has acquired the habit of cutting, on his recovery from these ailments he may be deemed to be SOUND.

REARING.

Rearing is a habit which horses acquire from their being used by nervous people, and by those who through ignorance of their real danger are deceived into believing themselves good horsemen. Rearing is taught by violence and by the improper or too violent use of sharp bits. The use of bits of this character often destroys the original courage of the horse, and renders him dangerous and good for nothing. Unlike most other vices of the horse, that of rearing is more dangerous to deal with in its earlier stages than when it has become confirmed; for, in the former case, the horse occasionally overbalances himself and falls upon his rider, while, in the latter, past experience teaches the horse to retain his equilibrium, although in such cases he does sometimes make mistakes.

No nervous person should attempt to use a rearing horse, as a very little mismanagement of the mouth will produce serious consequences,—that is to say, an inexperienced or careless rider may, by pulling a tight rein when he should give a loose one, throw the horse over on his back.

Rearing is not easily cured: it is a Vice.

JIBBING.

Horses acquire the habit of jibbing, by being mismanaged on their first essay in harness. They should then be treated with the greatest patience, however much time may be apparently wasted in getting them to start. Jibbing is curable.

The single jibber is not, on that account, dangerous, if he is not hurried, but is allowed to make his own start according to his humor.

Jibbing is dangerous, when the horse runs backward instead of forward; when he lies down; and when, at starting, he plunges forward: these latter three cases being aggravated forms of jibbing. Every form of jibbing is, however, a Vice.

RUNNING AWAY OR BOLTING.

Horses addicted to running away are decidedly dangerous, both for the user and for all that they encounter. This habit is the result of mismanagement, because no horse with a good mouth when well handled can run away.

The cure is not difficult to effect; but until that is effected, and the mouth restored to its proper condition, the horse is decidedly VICIOUS.

When bolting or running away is caused by defective vision, the vice is, properly so called, shying; although this is often, by misnomer, called bolting, on account of the difficulty experienced in pulling up, owing to the bad mouth.

A tendency of blood to the head, or any defect in the organs of vision, renders a horse UNSOUND.

BITING.

Biting to any serious extent is induced in the horse by the nervousness or thoughtlessness of its attendants; it is, however, a proof of ill-nature on the part of the horse, and a VICE.

But that pretty, half vengeful, half playful kind of snapping with the mouth, while the ears are whimsically laid back, and the laughing eyes shine with harmless mischievousness—the peculiarities of horses possessing a strain of Eastern blood—is no more a vice than is the gentle bite of a gambolling puppy. Neither is the habit of throwing out one of the hind legs in a careful manner—a habit peculiar to those horses—to be considered a vice. But ill-treatment and mismanagement will not fail to make such habits at length dangerous.

In those cases in which a horse is driven into doing wrong, such misconduct, until it has become a regular habit, is NOT VICE.

For if you flog, spur, or otherwise punish a horse till he acts wrongly, the fault is yours. All horses that are good for anything, will resent improper usage; and if you raise their mettle beyond your power of control, the blame lies with you, and not with the horse.

For the accomplishment of certain purposes with man, the excitement of his passions and feelings is sometimes successfully adopted; but an excess in this course frustrates the object, and the result is the reverse of what is desired.

The same is the case with the horse: by raising his passions to a certain pitch, you bring out the evidences of his high spirit in the most graceful action; but, if you venture a little too far, you raise in him a dangerous spirit of opposition—the more dangerous as such cases occur only to bad horsemen, who unfortunately depend entirely upon sheer strength for getting out of the difficulty; the natural consequence being that the horse is victorious, and from that and subsequent victories acquires a vice most difficult to cure.

Considering this subject of great importance, not only to the owner, but to the noble animal whose welfare every one acquainted with horses, cannot fail to have at heart, I dwell upon this subject in the hope of making proper treatment, and the consequences of ill-treatment, well understood by all—but especially by those who ignore the fact that it is possible to rouse a horse's temper beyond their own notion of what is right, even if that horse is not by nature vicious—and of proving to the most obtuse the absurdity, danger, and barbarity of excessive and improper punishment.

For it is but seldom that the horse requires correction, and even then mildness will, in most instances, accomplish your purpose.

Let, then, mercy go hand in hand with firmness and justice, always remembering that horses are not innately vicious: they derive whatever vice they ever have from the impolicy or cruelty of their users and attendants; but when any one bad trick thus acquired has become a confirmed bad habit, it is a VICE.

PRICE.

It is frequently believed, that when a certain price, varying in amount according to the different notions of different people, is paid for a horse, and that price is accepted by the vendor, a warranty is implied. The absurdity of such a conclusion is evident from what may be deduced from the preceding pages, inasmuch, as we have therein seen that most useful horses may fail to come up to the strict standard of soundness, while some of the most worthless and useless are strictly entitled to such a warranty.

This view is strengthened by the fact that, while no used or second-hand horse exists which has not a bar to a warranty for soundness, yet, not unfrequently, several thousand dollars are given for a horse on account of its well-known superior qualities and usefulness. A distinct kind of warranty for horses of this class is, therefore, a great desideratum.

A horse which, contrary to his natural normal condition, can seldom do one day's very hard work without for ever after bearing evidence thereof, can yet do an immense amount of work continuously for several years, in a satisfactory way, and free from lameness and other inconveniences. A horse, however, that has never done any work, but shows similar "structure" or symptoms, must be looked upon with suspicion, and ought to be called, as in most instances he is, UNSOUND.

The difference between the horse that has never been worked, and a used or worked one, is easily detected.

Horses that show signs of past work, yet perform the amount of labor due from one of their class, ought to be warranted as "worked horses."

Thus, when a worked horse is no longer qualified for the same kind of work as that which he has been accustomed to, or where he has such of the above-mentioned trifling drawbacks, as are not detrimental to his fulfilling his vocation, he should bear a warranty, at the very least, as a "used horse;" and where a worked horse becomes degraded to a lower class (as in the case of a horse which, no longer suitable for a hunter or saddle-horse, yet makes a very good harness-horse), he should be described in the warranty as a "used horse, for harness only."

By the largest users of this class of horse, this want is well known and much felt; and although legislation has not provided such a form of conditional warranty, yet it is frequently given and taken by stage-coach owners and others. The warranties, however, accepted by such persons, often allow too great laxity in the case of horses intended for ordinary purposes.

This is mentioned to show how easy it would be to frame such a warranty for used horses, as would benefit and satisfy both purchasers and vendors.

Three-fourths, at the least, of our hunters, though not, in strictness, entitled to it, do bear a warranty; and, in fact, as they do their work well, and may never have been lame, or if lame—lame for only a very short period—no one discovers in them any deviation from that standard of excellence which is implied in the magic word—"Warranted."

Where then is the harm of those supposed defects which causes no inconvenience to our saddle and other horses? Change of structure is not so much looked for or commented upon in the slower-going draught-horse, in whom such change of structure is produced more gradually, owing to the gentle pace at which he is generally worked. All that is expected of him being that he shall do his allotted work properly.

AGED HORSES.

Another plea in favor of a definite form of warranty for used horses is to be found in the facts—

1. That aged horses very rarely fulfill the conditions of warranty of unworked horses.

2. That, notwithstanding such defects, they are generally well qualified to do work required by the nervous, the timid, the elderly, and the indifferent horseman, as well as by those who, constantly requiring a great amount of work done at once, have yet no time to spare in carefully handling, or in regularly exercising their horses.

There certainly exists a senseless prejudice against buying such old horses; yet, every real horseman well knows the luxury of using a fine, active old horse, which cannot even be forced into doing wrong—the case with every horse that has, for a considerable time, been ridden by a true horseman. You must let him, for the most part, judge for himself; and you will find that his judgment is right.

Not less valuable is the old saddle horse, while the old harness horse knowingly measures the width of his wheels, and, on all occasions, takes his proper side of the road.

Well-seasoned old horses are less liable to disease than young ones, and do not tire so soon.

It is a mistake to suppose that young horses will last longer in work than old ones (provided that the latter have not been hard-worked while young), working against each other. The old one will work the young one off his legs; while with similar work the latter will succumb in a much shorter time, and unless great care, attention, and nursing are granted to him, and he is very regularly exercised, he will become troublesome and lose his health.

The old horse, on the contrary, comes out of his stable, after his rest, as staid and sober as ever.

I am aware that in advocating for particular purposes such superiority, I encounter the prejudice of all but true horsemen, who well know the valuable qualities of old horses. On the other hand, where you have time, and want your horses for ornament, you will find great pleasure in teaching young horses, in improving their mouths, and in promoting in them graceful action. But this should be attempted by those only who keep more than two horses, without which it is very difficult to do the young horses justice.

A further reason why the old horse suits many persons is, that when he is eight years old or more, and has never "been down," great reliance may be placed upon his being foot sure: he will never fall, until either the senile weakness of extreme old age comes upon him, or he becomes, from continuous hard work, leg-weary. In fact, such work as this will bring "down" any horse, whatever be his age or make.

By the time, too, that he has arrived at this age, greater dependence can be placed upon his eyesight; for all ravages made upon his eyes by disease are, at the completion of his eighth year, pretty well defined, so that they will thenceforth remain in their then condition, till work and time causes the pupils to dilate. Old horses, finally, are little apt to notice objects, even in the most trifling way, as there are few things that they have not previously seen and become accustomed to: and when they do meet anything strange and out of the common, they rarely shy, remembering how often they have been needlessly alarn

CLICKING—SHOVEL AND TONGS—POKER AND TONGS.

These terms are used to express the sound produced by, and show the existence of, over-reaching

OVER-REACHING.

Clicking, or striking the hind shoe against the fore one, while the horse is in action, often proceeds from his having been improperly ridden. As a warranty of soundness has nothing to do with what a horse has or has not been taught, so long as he is capable, with proper education, of doing the work due from one of his class, and, therefore, is not physically disqualified, he is   SOUND.

But when over-reaching or clicking is caused by his body being too short for his legs, or, as some express it, by his legs being too long for his body, the danger is much greater than in the former case; for, in this latter, he is much more liable to tread on the heel of the forefoot, and thus throw himself down, or tear off the forefoot shoe, in this instance, also running a great risk of falling. Such clicking stamps a horse as   UNSOUND.

He is sound so long as there is no abrasion or injury; but he requires careful shoeing and adapting to right work.

As long as any abrasion of the skin, or soreness of heel, arising from over-reaching, exists, the horse is

UNSOUND.

I will here say, that whatever may be the opinion, in such cases, as to soundness, short-bodiedness itself is a defect of so glaring a character, that a horse of the kind will be rarely palmed off for any but the meanest purposes.

Short-bodiedness, however, must not be confounded with "short back;" in fact, the back can hardly be too short.

YOUNG HORSES.

When young horses are, on the one hand, to be broken in, in the short space of time not uncommonly allotted by indifferent horsemen, so as to be fit to be ridden, such time not allowing the paces to become "set"; or when, on the other hand, they are worked at so early an age, that no notion can be formed of their capabilities, we cannot but foresee that they will come to some mischief or other.

As a somewhat analogous case, take that of a man brought from the farm, to be drilled in military exercises for a month or six weeks, and then to be allowed to go as he pleases, yet tied down to work totally different from that to which he has hitherto been accustomed; and then say how long it would be before he would return to his original gait and habits? Considering then the superiority of reason in man to that of the animal, can we fairly expect more of a horse than of a man?

The old soldier, long and well trained, and not subsequently overworked, forever afterwards retains somewhat of an erect, military air. The old horse, ridden for some years by a good horseman, must be seriously overworked if he do not show, by his well-trained gait and by the use of his haunches, evidences of good drill and education.

USED HORSES.

The used horse, as has been before remarked, may be sound—so he may show signs of having been well broken, and well trained, and yet not move in his old wonted easy and graceful style.

In such case, nothing but long-continued rest and good feeding will bring back the jaunty step and manner which he certainly once possessed. Recollecting great fatigues that he has undergone, and speculating on the probability of his having to exert all his powers, he carefully husbands his resources. He retains that manner of stepping with the least fatigue to himself, which experience has taught him.

LOW-ACTION, OR DAISY-CUTTING, OR GOING NEAR THE GROUND.

Fever in the feet produces in horses low and ungraceful action; until that is cured, the horse is UNSOUND.

When such low action is produced by the muscles being over-strained, until, by perfect rest, or by proper physicking, the horse is restored, he is UNSOUND.

But the manner of skimming over the ground peculiar to blooded horses, is sometimes a habit only, and not dangerous: so that, if this is not the result of disease, the horse is SOUND.

The above remarks refer only to extremely low action.

Action, on the contrary, may be too high for practical purposes; it is then frequently called "clambering."

STUMBLING.

Stumbling is often occasioned by inflammation of the feet arising from tightness of shoes, or from unequal pressure. A horse liable, from these causes, to stumble is UNSOUND.

In most instances, stumbling will vanish when the promoting cause is removed; and even when that cause is chronic inflammation of the feet, the disease may be greatly relieved, and the stumbling propensity much diminished.

It is here important to state that when a horse is cured, he is sound; for many persons allege that a horse, once unsound, is unsound for ever.

Certainly, there are some diseases that leave lasting traces; and, in such cases, although the disease be so far cured, that it no longer endangers the animal's life, or that, if it progress at all, it progresses only slowly, those traces of disease are sufficient to stamp the horse as
UNSOUND.

And where there has formerly been active disease in the feet, or where there is such a change of structure in any part as to interfere with his usefulness, he is
UNSOUND.

Acute fever frequently terminates in chronic disease, or the chronic form may have been produced gradually, lameness appearing and disappearing at short intervals; thus, while the horse is accused of shamming, the disease becomes confirmed before the real cause is suspected.

FEVER IN THE FEET.

Fever in the feet will produce in a horse "low action," or "going near the ground," and the horse thus afflicted is
UNSOUND.

If fever in the feet be of so recent a character as not to have caused an alteration in the structure of the feet, it is curable; but this disease is so rapid in its progress, and so quickly assumes a chronic form and produces permanent lameness, that it is rarely worth while buying a horse thus affected, unless you are thoroughly conversant with the treatment proper for such cases.

WATER.

Of the many promoting causes of fever in the feet, I will here mention one, and only one—the easiest of all to prevent. It is stinting the horse of water. Let the horse have all the water that he chooses to drink; do not stint him in the least; the water will do him no injury whatever, if he is not worked immediately after his first satisfying drink and he is watered sufficiently often afterwards. The number of times a day that he may want water depends on many and varying causes; but he should be watered so often that he will not care to drink more than four quarts at one time. Proportionately, that amount of water will not occupy so much space in his stomach as does half a pint of liquid in the stomach of a man. Some hardy horses will take the full allowance five times a day, while frequently weakly ones will not take the specified quantity, though watered only twice. Four times daily is little enough for any of them.

Cold water acts as a tonic to sick and weak horses, enabling them to eat more food, and, as they gain strength, to do more work.

The horse, when brought into the stable, is taken from soft, succulent, and cooling food, and deprived of the double privilege of drinking as much water as he chooses, and of taking his exercise when and how he likes on soft and cool ground, to be put upon dry, hard, stimulating food, regulated in amount; to be in, unfortunately, most cases, stinted in his supply of water; to be forced to work on hard dry roads, shod as he is, with iron shoes that become heated by the continuous friction they undergo; and, as a climax, to be placed, at the end of his involuntary labor, on a warm, dry floor, made still warmer by an overspread layer of straw. Need we, then, wonder that this extreme change of diet does produce such heat of body as, apart from the forced labor, is sufficient to produce decided disease.

THE HORSE.

Disease thus produced must necessarily settle in the weakest part; and whether such part be the battered feet, kept warm or dry, or any other part, such as the lungs, the liver, the eyes, etc., thither flies the malady.

WORK.

The straining produced by long-continued work causes horses to step in a low and ungraceful manner; but if they are not thereby prevented from doing their proper work conveniently, they are, nevertheless, SOUND.

But should they be disabled by past fatigue from working properly, they are UNSOUND.

In this case, if there is no chronic disease in them, good rest or a "run at grass" will effect a cure, and they are then, again, SOUND.

When horses, from long-continued fast work, go near the ground, so long as they can conveniently fulfill their proper tasks, they are SOUND.

But if unable, therefrom, to work properly, they are UNSOUND.

Where, however, no chronic disease exists, good rest, or turning out for awhile, may restore them and make them again SOUND.

It is well known that stage-coach horses capable of going at the rate of ten miles, and compelled to work at the rate of eight miles an hour, will, in a couple of years, be unable to do more than six; and yet a common observer would not detect in such horses any signs of their being "beat" or distressed; in fact, they may still be in good condition. This decrease in their powers, when caused by contraction of the fibre of the muscles (if there is no other injury or malady existing), can by proper rest be overcome, and such horses be restored to their original turn of speed.

In here naming the case of the stage-coach horse I certainly take an extreme case; besides, this class of horse is degraded from faster to slower work, according to his capabilities at the time, so long as he suits his proprietor's purpose. Many private horses also become greatly reduced in their powers of speed by careless and reckless driving; these latter can, by sufficient rest, coupled with slower driving and more careful usage, be gradually restored.

Thus, such horses as may, by rapid, careless, or unusually hard work, have been reduced in speed, but still be capable of restoration by care and rest proportionate to their particular class, should be entitled to be warranted as ' sound as used horses."

To many persons such horses would prove serviceable and profitable, and the horses be themselves saved a great deal of future misery; since, were the above facts better known, no inconsiderable number of such horses, requiring nothing but a little gentle usage and quiet rest, would be bought for work for which they were adapted, would eventually, and as a general thing, quickly recover, and would thereby escape the drudgery which only too often renders the rest of their lives burdensome and miserable.

NECK VEIN.

The irritation, which is sometimes occasioned in the neck vein by the punctures of the fleam or lancet in bleeding, not unfrequently extends to inflammation, which, beginning at the orifice of the puncture, progresses towards the head, and, if not subdued, obliterates the neck vein on that side. While this disease is in progress, from the time of the incision to its thorough determination, the horse is UNSOUND.

When the vein is at length destroyed, and the surrounding parts completely healed, the horse will not be impeded in doing his proper work, and will not require to have extra attention bestowed upon him. Any inconvenience that he may experience may arise from the lowering of his head in feeding off the ground when he is "at grass," as on such occasions an enlargement may be perceived at the junction of the head and neck, on the affected side. But as he does not show any signs of the swelling being unpleasant, as he does not demand extra care, as he continues to perform the proper work of his class, and, as the swelling vanishes soon after the head is raised, he is SOUND.

However, the loss of the vein, to prevent dispute, had better be mentioned.

The deprivation of this vein in a horse is a BLEMISH.

When the neck veins on both sides are destroyed, the horse may still be able to do his assigned work properly. Nature oftentimes finds beautiful substitutes for performing work that was intended to be done by apparatus which has been destroyed. But if he is turned out "at grass," and therefore forced to feed off the ground, he is likely to be choked; on that account, therefore, he requires more than the ordinary care required by horses of his class, and is consequently UNSOUND.

Where there is a liability to irritation in the neck vein, arising either from constitutional peculiarities, or from the horse's condition at the time, it is advisable to bleed from the leg vein; this latter vein should be the one selected to bleed from in those cases, also, in which the horse to be bled has already lost one of the neck veins.

LARGE BARREL.

A good, large, barrel-shaped body is evidence of a horse's possession of good health and powers of endurance; it is, therefore, a sign that he is SOUND.

But a distended, bulky stomach is, on the contrary, too often an indication of dropsy, in which case the horse is UNSOUND.

HERRING-GUTTED.

Herring-guttedness is the converse of large barrel, the horse being, in this case, small and straight in the body, and, generally, of a nervous and irritable disposition; he may, however, be SOUND.

But if this fretfulness of disposition renders the horse, as is very commonly the case, incapable of undergoing the amount of labor due from one of his class, he is then UNSOUND.

Medicine administered to the horse, either too frequently or in too severe doses, will, by producing chronic irritation of the bowels, induce herring-guttedness. This irritation accounts for the hot, nervous, fidgety temper generally evinced by small-barrelled horses. A horse thus suffering is UNSOUND.

When, inversely, the small barrel is the result of fretfullness and fidgety temper produced by cruel treatment, continued kindness, such as the horse has a natural right to expect, will soon restore him to good temper, and his barrel will resume its proper proportions; in this case the horse is SOUND.

When a horse is so hot-tempered as to be dangerous to ordinary users, if he has been warranted quiet for that particular kind of work in which he shows irritability, he may be returned on the score of breach of warranty, as his fault is a decided VICE.

HOT WATER.

The too frequent use of hot water, administered as a drink, produces a small barrel and general debility, and the horse becomes UNSOUND.

But, as hot or warm water is often of the highest service, it is the excessive use only of it that is to be condemned; we must, therefore, observe that it is not the proper use, but the abuse of this drink that is to be avoided.

WASHEY.

Washey is a term applied to a horse when the least exercise produces in him purging, the cause being irritation of the intestines: such a horse is small in the barrel. For the promoting causes of irritation of the intestines, see the article, "Herring-gutted."

A horse laboring under this malady is incapable of performing his work like others of his class, a very little exertion causing him great inconvenience, and he is, therefore, UNSOUND.

For the difference between washey and rumbling, see the article "Rumbling."

TUCKED UP.

Tucked up is another term applied to small-barrelled horses, and is a condition produced by various causes: it is generally applied to a small-barrelled horse while he shows that he is suffering from actual pain, either that which is incidental to the early stages of his recovery, or that which is caused by a spavin, a prick in the hind foot, acute disease, etc. Such a horse is UNSOUND.

See also the articles "Herring-gutted," "Washey," etc.

RUMBLING.

Rumbling—which is frequently but erroneously confounded with washey, upon the supposition that the noise proceeds from air or water being lodged in the intestines—is, in fact, a sound that proceeds from the sheath. Horses liable to rumbling are not thereby inconvenienced, and are, for the most part, good, round-barrelled horses, and　　　　　　　　　　　　　Sound.

The fact that mares never make this noise is a sufficient explanation of its origin.

TRIALS OF USED HORSES.

Whenever any doubt exists as to the soundness of "used horses," or as to their capacity for doing the requsite work without pain or inconvenience, a trial, in some cases extending over several days, should not be grudged. Sure a trial must of course be in strict accordance with the then condition of the horse to be tried; that is, the horse must be tried in that work only which can be expected from horses of that class in which his condition at the time showed him to be.

Paradoxical as it might at first sight appear, many an unused horse would, by being subjected to a used horse trial, be degraded by that very trial to this second class. See "Aged Horses."

I mention this to show what attention and care are required in the trial of a horse, and especially to prove that, while the slightest marks of having been submitted to even one day's work vitiate his title to a warranty of the first class, he is yet entitled to one of the second class: for all deviations from a natural state, whether such be the results of work, or of any other cause, debar him from a first-class warranty, but yet do not disqualify him for the performance of work. Then, if a doubt arise as to the power of such a horse, possessing as he does certain defects and blemishes, to do his proper work conveniently, the right course is to submit him to trial in his specific vocation, certain regulations and stipulations being beforehand agreed upon.

Thus, if the proposed purchase is warranted to be in hunting condition, a fair and moderate trial with hounds, or in other words, an ordinary day's hunt, is justifiable; and, if you cannot insure the company of the owner for this purpose, it is important to obtain his previous consent to the extreme test to which you propose to subject the horse.

For a real and experienced horseman, a short trial suffices; for he knows well the state of condition that the horse under trial requires to qualify him for his work, and the necessity for making ample allowance for any apparent defect.

STOPPING.

Some horses have a trick of suddenly stopping, or pulling up short, when going at a fast pace. A horse of this kind is dangerous, from the likelihood of his throwing moderate riders over his head: such a trick is a
VICE.

This trick is additionally dangerous, because a horse that has this habit, will, probably, if hastily urged on to start afresh, begin some other trick. If this habit is not of very recent growth, it is very difficult to cure, requiring a true horseman's vigilance and patience: the horse is, however, SOUND.

But where disease of the eyes is the cause of this habit, no cure can be effected until the disease is removed, and, in the interim, the horse is UNSOUND.

TURNING.

Turning, that is, sudden and improper turning or twisting round, is a dangerous and troublesome habit; when it is not caused by disease, it is a VICE.

But if, upon examination of the eyes of the horse, you find them to be diseased or injured, you must then treat him, not as vicious, but as UNSOUND.

STIFF HOCKS.

Some horses are naturally stiffer and less elastic than others in the movements of the hocks. It is only by the stiffness of these propellers—*cæteris paribus*—that a horse is prevented from being the fastest of his kind.

There are, therefore, relative degrees of perfection of horses in this respect; so that, where the degree of elasticity is insufficient for one species of work, it may yet be suited to work of another kind, so long as such comparative stiffness does not inconvenience the horse; and the buyer has every opportunity for ascertaining whether the "paces" of his proposed purchase are suitable for the labor required.

Stiff or naturally slow hocks do not prevent the horse from being declared SOUND.

Where, however, as in the articles "Spavin" and "Curb," such stiffness is caused by disease, the horse is UNSOUND.

HARD MOUTH.

The mouth being so hard as to render the horse unmanageable by ordinary users is a VICE.

But to this rule there is a well-known exception in the case of "trotters," which are expected to run away in trotting, and which, from their make, as before described, must bear heavily on the bit, so as to be kept upon their legs. With this class of horses, a hard mouth is considered rather a virtue.

This expression—hard mouth—often misleads users into treating a horse as if he had altogether lost all sensation in his mouth, thereby aggravating instead of remedying the evil; the fact being, that mismanagement has drilled the horse into bearing unnecessary punishment of the bit—while a good horseman will quickly make the horse answer his hand, and in a short time permanently restore the tone and liveliness of its mouth.

WOUNDS.

Wounds of every description, however slight they may be, since there is no certainty as to how they may terminate, stamp a horse as UNSOUND.

ABRASIONS.

Very slight abrasions, though scarcely attracting notice, and requiring little if any special care, yet, for the time being, stamp the horse as UNSOUND.

Should abrasions, however, occur on any joint, such as the knee, etc., or any other important part, as gravel may have worked in, and the bruise be, consequently, serious, additional attention is called for. In this case the horse is decidedly UNSOUND.

But when the abrasion is perfectly healed, he is SOUND.

BALD PLACES.

Bare or bald places, which occur on many parts of horses' bodies, are not deserving of much notice, not being indications of any fault, nor of any liability to accidents.

However, when they are accounted unsightly, they are considered to be   BLEMISHES.

With a saddle-horse such a blemish, occurring on the shoulders, is decidedly unsightly; while, in a harness-horse otherwise suitable for the purpose, it would be ridiculous to object to that which is covered by the collar. The same reasoning applies to the marks beneath the roller or saddle, as well as to all such as are covered by the horse's trapping when at work.

BLEMISHES.

All scars left from wounds or sores, as well as all unsightly enlargements, whether such be the effects of blows, work, or sprains, are blemishes.

Some blemishes do and some do not impair the horse's value: thus, while collar-marks are considered a disgrace to a saddle-horse, and lessen his value, in a very superior harness-horse they would be altogether overlooked.

Broken knees lessen the market price of all horses. So, also, does the loss of one or both eyes.

Marks on the fetlock show that the horse has, at some time or other, cut, and therefore require to be noticed with a view to seeing what probability there is that he will do so again. But if such marks are not the result of any peculiarity in his make, they may be, perchance, of no consequence, as it is possible they may have been produced in him when, as a colt, he was being broken, or when subsequently, he was laboring under severe illness, fatigue, or want of condition.

The observations here made are intended merely to assist in deciding the relative bearing and importance of blemishes in general, each particular one being treated of in its proper place in this work.

GALLS.

Galls are injuries arising from some part of the horse's furniture, such as the collar, saddle, etc.

SADDLE-BACK—CRADLE-BACK—HOLLOW-BACK—LOW-BACK.

Saddle-back, cradle-back, hollow-back, and low-back, are terms used to denote the form of a horse who has his back lower than in ordinary cases.

Such a horse, when not so low in the bend of the back as to be disqualified for carrying a fair amount of weight, is generally easy and pleasant to ride, and   SOUND.

But, when the back is so low that the horse cannot carry proper weight, though he may be a good harness-horse, he is, as a saddle-horse,   UNSOUND.

For harness such a horse may be considered sound, and he is by some preferred for his showing an elevated forehand.

ROACH-BACK—HIGH-BACK.

Roach or high-back is the inverse of low-back, and is frequently produced in a horse by his being set to draw heavy weights while he is young. When it occurs to a moderate extent only, it does not impede him in his work, and he is, therefore,   SOUND.

Even though it does not interfere with his title to a warranty of soundness, yet, when it is a positive disfigurement to the horse, it is held to be a   BLEMISH.

When the back is weakened, or the horse is thereby impeded in his work, he is   UNSOUND.

COLLAR-WRUNG.

So long as the collar-wrung horse is sore, and until the raw part is completely healed, and covered with skin, he is UNSOUND.

When the sore is thoroughly covered with new skin, he is SOUND.

But the bald place or mark showing the site of the former injury is a BLEMISH.

Should the horse be intended for harness-work, and the mark be neither too high nor too low to be covered by a well-fitting collar, it is hardly worth while to take particular notice of so trivial a blemish concealed as it is, especially if the horse be quite free from inconvenience, and be, in all other respects, suited to your purpose.

From the size of the blemish it is conspicuous and unsightly in a saddle horse; besides, you must remember that the same mark which is hidden by the winter's coat, often reappears in all its ugliness when the horse is clipped, and when he changes his coarser coat for the finer gloss of summer.

BLEEDING.

Bleeding, simple as the operation seems, and in spite of the careless and slovenly manner in which many horse owners allow it to be performed, is not unattended with danger.

As mischievous and unexpected results follow from even the most carefully-executed operation, until the orifice made by the lancet or fleam is completely healed, the horse is UNSOUND.

When he is healed, and no evil effects or symptoms remain, he is SOUND.

See article on "Neck-vein."

Any large unsightly knot or lump about the neck-vein will generally be found to be the effect of bleeding, and must be considered a BLEMISH.

SCARS.

See "Wounds" and "Blemishes."

FIRING.

It is not advisable here to discuss the merits or demerits of firing, as deep or severe firing is seldom resorted to.

When the horse has been subjected to such an ordeal, however neatly the operation may have been performed, the mark, which will remain as long as he lives, must be held to be a BLEMISH.

Such is not the case, however, with superficial firing, as then, in most cases, the traces are scarcely perceptible; therefore, except in rare instances, these slight traces do not constitute a BLEMISH.

If, after firing, the horse goes free from lameness and inconvenience, the disease being completely removed and with the exception of the scars resulting from the operation no alteration of structure having taken place, he is SOUND.

NERVOUSNESS.

Nervousness or fidgetiness in the horse's disposition to such an extent as to render him difficult to clean, harness, saddle, bridle, or put into the stable, or as to make him jump or start at any unaccustomed noise or sight in or out of the stable, is a VICE.

Although this fidgetiness and restlessness are generally caused by the mismanagement or thoughtlessness of the attendants, proper treatment will restore the horse to tranquility and usefulness. But none but an accomplished horseman should venture to possess such a horse until it is cured of such habits, as the nervousness or ignorance of the rider will only render the horse worse, and drive him into a dangerous state of desperation.

LAMPAS.

Lampas is a fullness in the mouth of young horses and is so generally confined to them as to be almost an incontrovertible proof of youth.

If lampas interferes with their eating, a little blood should be taken away by scarifying the roof of the mouth, or a dose of physic should be administered. Until one of these two courses is adopted, the horse is UNSOUND.

As soon as the bleeding in the mouth is finished, and the wound healed, or the medicine has worked off, the horse will feed as well as ever, and is SOUND.

This complaint would hardly be worth so much notice if it were not for the barbarous and cruel practice, too commonly resorted to, of burning out or cauterizing, and so putting the animal to much unnecessary pain, preventing him during several days from eating, and magnifying a scarcely noticeable triviality into a matter of consequence.

Another bad effect of cautery is the premature shrinking or withering of the gums, thereby giving the horse an appearance of age greater than is really the case; for the teeth do not, either in man or quadrupeds, grow longer as age advances, but the gums, as they recede, leave exposed a larger portion of the teeth, which thereby apparently increase in length. In addition to this, the teeth, when no longer maintained firmly in their places by the gums, begin to fall out, and so give an apparent but false confirmation of the supposition of old age.

Besides the false appearance of age that cautery gives, premature decrepitude and its attendant ills are to be feared and avoided; for, that such ills must follow, is sufficiently clear when we consider how certain it is that the powers of digestion and mastication are impaired if not lost when the teeth are gone.

This shows the importance of not unnecessarily reducing the fullness of the mouth.

WALL-EYES.

According to popular rumor wall-eyes never become blind, though how this error has originated it is difficult to see.

The appearance peculiar to wall-eyes is due to the absence of the coloring matter of the iris, and therefore, were it true that the colored eye alone was liable to blindness, wall-eyes would be the only sound ones; and, in such case, He who has arranged with perfect wisdom everthing for the good of His creatures would have made them the most prevalent, and not the exception.

The truth is that such eyes are neither weaker nor stronger than ordinary ones, and are, therefore, SOUND.

And wall-eyes are not considered a BLEMISH.

WHITE OF EYES.

A horse that usually shows much white of the eye, particularly at the front corner, or that nearer to the nose, is, in most cases, hasty and nervous, if not violent, and you may believe, accustomed to ill usage.

In exceptional instances you will find a mild-tempered horse showing much of the white, owing to the unusual smallness of the iris, but the difference of expression in the two cases is most apparent, the one expressing rage or fear, while the other beams with mildness and confidence.

EXCHANGE.—SWAP.

In an exchange, or, as it is technically termed, in a swap, it is vulgarly believed that no warranty, given by either party to the transaction, is binding.

Absurd as this may appear, I am not aware that the question has ever been decided judicially; and I will, therefore, mention the method adopted by those who affect to be aware of this singularity.

A gives B a receipt for two hundred dollars, and a cheque for one hundred, and receives B's horse; while B gives A a receipt for three hundred dollars, and takes A's horse, A having agreed with B to value their horses at, respectively, two hundred and three hundred dollars.

Then A imagines that, should the horse which he has taken of B not fulfill the terms of the warranty, he can recover his three hundred dollars; and equally satisfied is B that, if the warranty which he has received from A is not verified to the letter, he will get his two hundred dollars returned; or the one imagines that, in such case, he may compel the other to a re-exchange, so as to place both A and B in the same position as that in which they were prior to the transaction.

I do not myself see why a warranty given in a swap or exchange should be void, especially when a money consideration is given and received. But, as it is advisable to avoid litigation as far as possible, I would suggest that, in an exchange, each party to the contract should hold a warranty in writing from the other, the value set upon the horse being marked thereon.

PARALYSIS.

The loss of the use of any limb or function, through injury to the brain, the nerves, or the muscles, is paralysis.

Horses laboring under a liability to this disease are, on some occasions, deprived instantaneously of the use of the part so affected; as, for example, a horse will become paralyzed in his leg while he is in action. I have known horses, while trotting or galloping rapidly, to be deprived momentarily of the use of a leg to the great risk of the rider, and, after a few moments, to recover the use as suddenly, and proceed as well as ever, until again attacked. A horse liable to paralysis is   Unsound.

Until this disease has endured long enough to shrink or partially wither the muscles, it is not easily detected by those who are not conversant with the symptoms.

Paralysis must not be associated with "shrunk muscles" when the muscles are shrunk from other causes.

HUMORS.

Humor is a term applied to swelling of the legs and other parts of the horse, and to small spots on the body which denote a want of medicine or bleeding. When humor arises from weakness or overwork, tonics should be applied occasionally, but as they are not popularly understood by the term medicine, it is right they should be mentioned to prevent the substitution of depletents.

A horse while thus troubled is   Unsound.

When the effect of the medical treatment is over, and the indication of its necessity removed, he is again Sound.

See article on "Surfeit."

CLAMBERING.

The high and short stepping of a horse is called clambering.

Clamberers are slow and, from the great waste of muscular energy, are but poor workers; they are in this respect, however, SOUND.

HIGH HIPS.

High hips are very unsightly; they owe their prominence to narrowness of the loins, and are therefore weak; high-hipped horses are long in the waist, that is, they are too lengthy from the hip to the last rib; they are inclined to be washy, and purge when exercised or sharply worked, and are frequently hot and colicky in temper.

All large-hipped horses are good leapers, on account of the great leverage provided by their wide hips, and are, in this respect, SOUND.

Where the loins are good, not flat sided, and "well ribbed home," the wider the hips the greater the horse's power; in such case the angularity is softened and the horse is a very superior one for work.

NARROW LOINS.

Narrow and weak loins are generally found with narrow hips, the defectiveness in this case being even worse than in that of high hips; but as the two defects generally go together, I refer to the article on "High Hips." Narrow-loined horses are SOUND.

LONG WAIST.

Long waist is a term applied to horses that are very lengthy between the last rib and the haunch-bone: such horses are weakly, have, generally, small loins, but are, so far, SOUND.

See the preceding two articles.

WIDE BEHIND.

Horses that spread or straddle their hind-legs when in fast action usually do so to prevent treading on the fore-feet, their shoulders being too upright to allow the fore-feet to be thrown forward sufficiently to be out of reach of the hind ones. They are seldom good travellers. Their hocks are generally skewed or "cow-hocked," and supposed to be weaker and more subject to disease. Unless, however, it amounts to an extreme malformation, they are SOUND.

But when they go wide owing to stiff or diseased hocks, they are UNSOUND.

See article on "Upright Shoulders."

DISHING.

Dishing is a term used to express the movements of those horses which turn out their fore-feet when in action; they usually lift their legs high and are safe to ride, but unpleasant, partly on account of the peculiar roll of the shoulders, and also because their action bespatters riders with mud.

This action is sometimes induced by bad breaking; with work it generally leaves horses, or as they get stronger with age they lose the habit.

A horse that thus turns his feet is unable to perform long journeys or to do extraordinary work, on account of the amount of exertion consumed in accomplishing the useless labor.

Horses that have this habit may still be considered SOUND.

PIGEON-TOED.

Horses that stand with the fronts of the hoofs turned towards each other are called pigeon-toed.

They are commonly considered to be unsafe, but this depends upon the width of chest, and upon whether they can or cannot perform all their paces without the toes of one foot touching the other leg so as to interfere with the usefulness of their action.

If this peculiarity, then, does not make them defective in the execution of their proper work, they are SOUND.

Of this I have known many instances amongst extraordinarily good horses.

But, should the peculiarity impede them in their labor, they are UNSOUND.

COCK-THROTTLED.

Horses that are stiff at the setting on of the head to the neck are termed cock-throttled.

They cannot bring their noses in properly, and are unpleasant to ride, from their not giving way with that elasticity which is required by the horseman's hand, but yet are SOUND.

When this defect is not cock-throttle proper, but is produced by sore throat, by a swelling of the vicinal glands, by severe cold, or by the commencement of strangles, the stiffness being occasioned by actual disease, the horse is UNSOUND.

INDEX.

	PAGE
Abrasions	118
Age	81
Aged Horses	103
Artificial Contraction	25
Asthma	63
Back, broken	53
" chinked	52
" cradle	120
" high	120
" hollow	120
" low	120
" roach	120
" saddle	120
Bald places	118
Bandages	33
Bar shoes	30
Bastard Strangles, or Vives	91
Bearing-Rein	57
Bent before	92
Biting	99
Bleeding	72, 121
Blemishes	119
Blindness, total	22
Blood Spavin	44
Bog Spavin	45
Bolting—Running away	84, 99
Boots	97
Broken Back	53
Canker	32
Capped Hocks	40
Chinked Back	52
Clambering	126
Clicking—Shovel and Tongs—Poker and Tongs	105
Coat, staring	47
Cock-throttled	129
Colds	62, 89
Collar-wrung	121
Contraction, artificial	25
Corns	26
Cough	62
Cough, chronic	62
Courage	50
Cradle-back	120
Crib-biting	63
" prevention of	63
Curbs	37
Cutting	48
Daisy-cutting	107
Dealers' Horses	73
Diet and Exercise	73

	PAGE
Dishing	128
Dropping before	54
Dropping behind	53
Dullness	68
Eating Beds	64
Enlargements, soft	96
Examination	15
Exchange—Swap	125
Exercise and Diet	73
Eyes, the	20
" wall	124
" white of	124
False Quarter	28
Feet, contracted	23
" contraction of the	15
" fever in the	108
Firing	122
Fleshy Heel	55
Foot, flat	17
" perfect	17
Galls	120
Glanders	89
Grease	46
Groggy	40
Grunting	60
Harness, quiet in	81
Hard Mouth	117
Heel, fleshy	55
Heels, cracked	46
Height and Age	81
Herring-gutted	113
High-back	120
Hip, low	46
Hips, high	127
Hocks	36
" capped	40
Hollow-back	120
Hoofs, open	17
Horse, the sound	66
" aged	103
" dealers'	73
" saddle	74
" used	106
" trial of	115
" young	106
Hot Water	113
Humors	126
Hunters	74
Jibbing	98
Joints, enlarged	96
" other Diseases of	46

INDEX.

	PAGE
Knees, the	18
Knees, broken	19
" swollen	20
Knuckling	93
Lame	41
Lameness	54
" cunning	55
Lampas	123
Large Barrel	112
Leather Soles	31
Legs, swollen	47
Loins, narrow	127
Long Pasterns	96
Long Waist	127
Low Action or Daisy-cutting, or going near the Ground	107
Low-back	120
Low Hip	46
Malformations	69
Medicine	73, 86
Mouth, hard	107
" the	22
Narrow Loins	127
Neck Vein	111
Nervousness	122
Open Hoofs	17
Over-reaching	105
Paralysis	125
Pasterns, long	96
Pigeon-toed	129
Play—Playfulness	84
Poker and Tongs	105
Price	101
Pumice Sole	18
Quiet in Harness	81
Rat Tail	49
Rearing	97
Receipts on Warranty	79
Rheumatism	43
Ring Bones	31
Roach-back	120
Roaring	60
Rumbling	114
Running away—Bolting	84, 99
Saddle Horses	74
Saddle-back Cradle-back, Hollow-back, Low-back	120
Sand-crack	27
Scars	122
Shoulders, upright	92
Shovel and Tongs	105
Shying	82

	PAGE
Sinews	59
Skittishness	86
Soft Enlargements	96
Spavin, blood	44
" bog	45
Spavins	38
Speedy-cut	34
Splents	33
Staring Coat	47
Starting	84
Stiff Hocks	117
Stopping	116
Strangles	88
String Halt	45
Stumbling	107
Surfeit	72
Swap	125
Thorough Pins	44
Thrushes	29
Trial, the	69
Trials of Used Horses	115
Tucked-up	114
Turning	116
Unnerving	49
Upright Joints—Knuckling	93
Upright Shoulders	92
Used Horses	106
" trial of	115
Vein, neck	111
Vices	76
Vives	91
Waist, long	127
Wall-Eyes	124
Warranties, Receipts on	79
Warranty	13
Warranty, use of	13
Washey	114
Water	109
Water, hot	113
Weaving	67
Weaving, cure of	68
Wens	47
Wheezing	62
Whistling	61
White of Eyes	124
Wide behind	128
Wind, broken	59
Wind-sucking	67
Windgalls	22
Work	110
Wounds	118
Young Horses	106

www.ingramcontent.com/pod-product-compliance
Lightning Source LLC
Chambersburg PA
CBHW020109170426
43199CB00009B/466